Beginner Classical Piano Music

Teach Yourself How to Play Famous Piano
Pieces by Bach, Mozart, Beethoven
& the Great Composers

Includes Streaming Videos!

Damon Ferrante

Book, Streaming Videos & MP3 Audio

Introduction: How the Book & Videos Work

As a piano professor and piano teacher for over twenty five years, I have wanted to help beginner piano students succeed in playing famous and beautiful music by the great composers. In the past, piano books on the great composers have taken a dull and uninspiring approach. Most of the time these books just throw together pieces by composers in a random, boring, and confusing way; sometimes these books are no better than blurry photocopies.

This book and video course takes a new and innovative approach!

Beginner Classical Piano Music makes learning great classical piano pieces fun, easy, interactive, and engaging. The book and streaming videos follow a step-by-step lesson format for learning some of the most famous music by Bach, Mozart, Beethoven, Pachelbel, Chopin, Tchaikovsky, Brahms, Liszt, Schumann, Dvorák, and many more great composers. Pieces you have always dreamt about playing on the piano for yourself and for your family and friends!

In *Beginner Classical Piano Music,* each lesson builds on the previous one in a clear and easy-to-understand manner. No music reading is necessary. I walk you through how to play these wonderful pieces, starting with very easy music, at the beginning of the book, and advancing, little by little, as you master new repertoire and techniques. As you are able to play these new pieces, you will also greatly improve your abilities on the piano! Along the way, you will learn to read music, play chords and scales, learn rhythms, techniques, and music theory, as well.

If you have always wanted to play famous pieces by the great composers, then, this book is for you. Let's get started on this exciting musical journey!

The Videos

This symbol means that there is a video lesson that corresponds to the material presented on the lesson page. These video lessons cover the concepts presented and also give instruction and tips on how to play certain famous pieces from the book.

To access the video lessons, go to steeplechasemusic.com and click on the link at the top of the page for Piano Books. Then, from the Piano Books webpage, click on the image for this book, "Beginner Classical Piano Music". On the webpage for Beginner Classical Piano Music, you will see a link to Video Lessons. Click that link for the Video Lessons webpage for this book. The video lessons are free and there is no limit on the number of times you may watch them.

Here is a list of some of the <u>Great</u> <u>Pieces</u> that you will learn in this book:

- Beethoven's *Für Elise*
- J.S. Bach's *Prelude in C Major*
- Mozart's *Turkish Rondo*
- Pachelbel's *Canon*
- Tchaikovsky's *Nutcracker*
- Liszt's *Hungarian Dance*
- Brahms' *Lullaby*
- Mendelssohn's *Wedding March*
- Strauss's *The Blue Danube Waltz*
- Grieg's *Hall of the Mountain King*
- Handel's *Hallelujah*
- Dvořák's *New World Symphony*
- Chopin's *Prelude*
- Bizet's *The Toreador Song*
- Verdi's *La donna è mobile*
- Schumann's *The Wild Horseman*
- Paganini's *Caprice Number 24*
- Beethoven's *Ode to Joy*
- Tchaikovsky's *Swan Lake*
- Mozart's *Eine kleine Nachtmusik*
- Mascagni's *Intermezzo* from *Cavalleria Rusticana*
- Offenbach's *Tales of Hoffmann*
- Gluck's *Orfeo ed Euridice*
- Erik Satie's *Gymnopedie*
- *Greensleeves*
- Rossini's *William Tell Overture*
  (The Theme from the *Lone Ranger*)

Table of Contents

Section 1: Introduction and Review of Basic Music Concepts

Page:

Section 2: Famous Pieces by Great Composers

Table of Contents for The Video Lessons

Important!

To access the video lessons, go to steeplechasemusic.com and click on the link at the top of the page for Piano Books. Then, from the Piano Books webpage, click on the image for this book, "Beginner Classical Piano Music". On the webpage for Beginner Classical Piano Music, you will see a link to Video Lessons. Click that link for the Video Lessons webpage for this book. The video lessons are free and there is no limit on the number of times you may watch them.

Getting Started

The inspiration for this book came from helping people who have dreamt of playing these famous pieces of classical music, but who haven't known where to begin. Over the last few decades of playing and teaching the piano, I have picked up a few helpful pointers that I would like to share with you at the beginning of the book:

1. One of the most important aspects for learning an instrument is cultivating a positive attitude. If you approach learning the piano with a happy, fun-loving spirit your mind and body will be much more receptive to learning new ideas. Having a can-do, positive outlook will not only make the process of learning more fun, but it has been proven to speed up the process of improving. So, you should always approach your piano playing as an exciting and rewarding activity of your day.

2. Another important aspect of playing the piano is forming good practice habits. Learning the piano is a fun and creative endeavor; if you develop good practice habits you will make rapid progress with your playing. This will require a little bit of focus and a proactive attitude on your part. However, it will make a big difference for you.

   Ideally, you should strive to practice around five to seven times per week (once per day) for about 20 to 40 minutes. If you have more time, that's great. However, it's best to spend your time practicing well (in an organized manner), rather than just spending a lot of time practicing. Along these lines, one of the most important facets of learning to play the piano is having some continuity in your practice routine. So, even on days that you are extremely busy, try to take 10-15 minutes to work on your piano playing. As best as you can, try to avoid missing more than three days of practicing in a row.

3. Have patience and a longterm perspective: You are embarking on a grand and lifelong adventure in music. Through this journey, you will discover new perspectives on sound, communication, friendship, success, coordination, self confidence, concentration, memory, and determination. For the most part, this learning will be a step-by-step process, where your ability and understanding of music will move ahead at a gradual pace. At other times, your progress may suddenly leap ahead to another level in a flash of inspiration.

Whatever your goals in music may be, it's best to cultivate an attitude that music is a lifelong journey and process of creating and developing. As an artist, you should continue to explore and develop your musical voice. Life will take you along different paths and these will be reflected in your music making. Enjoy this adventure, especially if you are just beginning. You are like some explorer stepping onto the deck of your ship heading out from your land's port to find yet-unexplored, new places. Enjoy the journey!

4. Lastly, a lot of beginning musicians overlook the importance of practicing with a metronome. A metronome is a mechanical or electronic device that keeps a steady beat. You can change the speed of the beats, which in music is called the "tempo", on all metronomes to allow for slower or faster pulses of rhythm.

As soon as possible, you should incorporate a metronome into your practicing for these piano pieces. This will help build and solidify your internal rhythm.

You can find a number of free or inexpensive metronome apps online. These will work on your computer, tablet, and smartphone. There are also a wide assortment of digital metronomes that you can purchase. Many of these can be found online or at your local music store for around ten dollars.

Damon Ferrante

GOOD NEWS: BONUS LESSONS!

This edition of *Beginner Classical Piano Music* includes free, bonus lessons.

1. Go to the Home Page of SteeplechaseMusic.com.

2. At the top of the Home Page, you will see a link for <u>Piano Books</u>.

3. Follow the link to the <u>Piano Books</u> webpage.

4. Then, click on the <u>Cover / Link</u> for *Beginner Classical Piano Music*.

5. Once you are on the webpage for the *Beginner Classical Piano Music*, click <u>MP3 Audio File Download</u> and download the PDF and MP3 Audio Files

Steeplechase Music Books

Also by Damon Ferrante

Piano Scales, Chords & Arpeggios Lessons with Elements of Basic Music Theory: Fun, Step-By-Step Guide for Beginner to Advanced Levels (Book & Videos)

Guitar Adventures: Fun, Step-By-Step Guide to Beginner Guitar (Book & Videos)

Guitar Scales Handbook: A Step-By-Step, 100-Lesson Guide to Scales, Music Theory, and Fretboard Theory (Book & Videos)

Guitar Adventures for Kids: Fun, Step-By-Step, Beginner Lesson Guide to Get You Started (Book & Videos)

Beginner Rock Guitar Lessons: Instruction Guide (Book & Videos)

Ultimate Guitar Chords, Scales & Arpeggios Handbook: 240-Lesson, Step-By-Step Guitar Guide, Beginner to Advanced Levels (Book & Videos)

Beginner Classical Piano Music:
Teach Yourself How to Play Famous Piano Pieces by Bach, Mozart, Beethoven and the Great Composers (Book, Streaming Videos & MP3 Audio)

by Damon Ferrante

For additional information about music books, recordings, and concerts, please visit the Steeplechase website: www.steeplechasemusic.com

Steeplechase Arts

ISBN-13: 978-0692823194
ISBN-10: 0692823190

Section 1: Introduction & Review of Basic Music Concepts

Section 1: Introduction and Review of Basic Music Concepts

Section 1 of this book serves as a review of basic music and piano concepts or as an introduction to these ideas for readers who are just beginning to play the piano for the first time. The focus of Section 1, which is about thirty-one pages, is to present some of these beginner-level piano fundamentals, like the finger numbers, names of the notes, the treble and bass clefs, counting and rhythm, and playing with both hands. If you have some experience playing the piano already and can read music, you may want to glance over the lessons in this section as a brief review, before starting on Section 2: Famous Pieces by Great Composers. If you are new to the piano or are not familiar with these concepts, take your time with the lessons in Section 1; they will provide you with a good foundation for playing the music in Section 2.

Although there are some pieces of music in Section 1, the primary goal for this section is to refresh your memory about basic music concepts or introduce you to them, if you are new to the piano. Interspersed throughout Section 1, there are excerpts of famous pieces for the right hand, left hand, or hands together. There are also exercises to help you practice rhythm, counting, learning the notes on the keyboard, and playing with both hands at the same time. Some of the pieces included in Section 1 are easier versions of pieces that will also appear in Section 2.

The Video Lessons:

This symbol means that there is a video lesson that corresponds to the material presented on the lesson page. These video lessons cover the concepts presented and also give tips on how to play certain famous pieces from the book.

To access the video lessons, go to steeplechasemusic.com and click on the link at the top of the page for Piano Books. Then, from the Piano Books webpage, click on the image for this book, "Beginner Classical Piano Music". On the webpage for *Beginner Classical Piano Music*, you will see a link to Video Lessons. Click that link for the Video Lessons webpage for this book. The video lessons are free and there is no limit on the number of times you may watch them.

1

Getting Started: An Overview of the Notes on the Keyboard

- The White Keys on the piano follow an alphabetic pattern that goes from A to G. In other words, this is the pattern: A, B, C, D, E, F, G.
- This pattern starts at the bottom (low bass notes) of the piano keyboard and repeats many times as the notes go upward and get higher in pitch ("sound").
- With your RH ("Right Hand") Index Finger, find the "A" key just 2 keys below MIddle C (See the Chart below). Move your Index Finger up (to the right) one key at a time. Try saying the letters as you press down each key.

Check out video 1

Down (Lower Pitch) ⟵——⟶ Up (Higher Pitch)

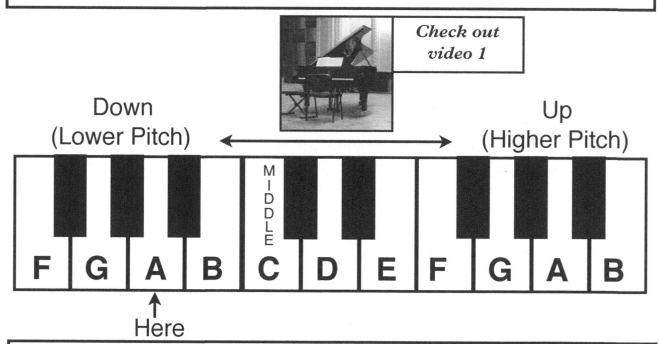

Here

- It is a good idea to associate each key with some object and imagine the object on top of the key. This will help you remember the name and location of each key.
- For this exercise, let's image that the piano keyboard is a table with food on it. The food, on this imagined table, will be placed in a set order going from left to right (See the chart below). Find the key "A" below Middle C and name the foods as you move upward (right). When you get to the second key "A", the pattern will repeat. Repeat this exercise.

White Keys Exercise: A= Apple, B= Bread, C= Cheese, D= Dessert, E= Eggs, F= Fish, G= Grapes

Exercises:
- Try Locating Middle C with Finger #1 (Thumb) of your Right Hand (RH)
- Try Locating Middle C with Finger #1 (Thumb) of your Left Hand (LH)
- Try Locating D with Finger #2 (Pointer Finger) of your Right Hand (RH)
- Try Locating E with Finger #3 (Middle Finger) of your Right Hand (RH)

2

An Overview of Counting and Measures

Check out video 2

- Music is composed of groups of beats called measures.
- Measures are set off by vertical lines, called bar lines.
- Measures most commonly contain 2, 3, or 4 beats.
- Below, are examples of sets of four measures in 4/4 time.
- In 4/4 time, you will count 4 beats for each measure.
  In other words, you will count: 1234, 1234, 1234, 1234.
- Try counting aloud and clapping the beats for the exercise below.

Example 1:

| 1 2 3 4 | 1 2 3 4 | 1 2 3 4 | 1 2 3 4 |

Example 2:
Try Clapping on the X: On the First Beat.

| 1 2 3 4 | 1 2 3 4 | 1 2 3 4 | 1 2 3 4 |
| X | X | X | X |

Example 3:
Try Clapping on the X: On the First and Third Beats.

| 1 2 3 4 | 1 2 3 4 | 1 2 3 4 | 1 2 3 4 |
| X X | X X | X X | X X |

Example 4:
Try Clapping on the X: On the Second Beat.

| 1 2 3 4 | 1 2 3 4 | 1 2 3 4 | 1 2 3 4 |
| X | X | X | X |

An Overview of Hand Position & Finger Numbers

- To create a good hand position for piano playing is easy. With both hands, imagine that you are holding an apple (with your palms facing upward and your fingers curved). Then, turn your palms to the floor and keep your fingers curved. **See Video Lesson 1**
- For piano playing, our fingers are given numbers. The numbers are the same for both hands. **See Video Lesson 1**

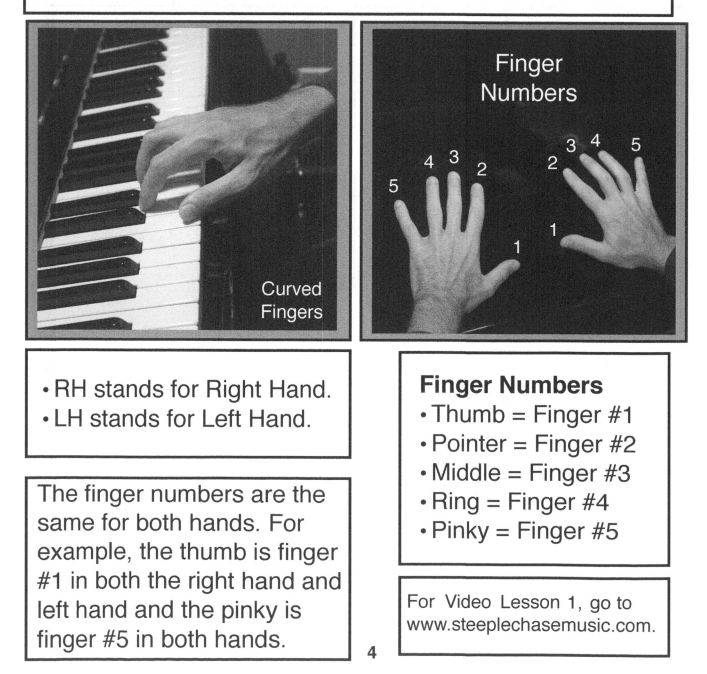

Curved Fingers

Finger Numbers

- RH stands for Right Hand.
- LH stands for Left Hand.

Finger Numbers
- Thumb = Finger #1
- Pointer = Finger #2
- Middle = Finger #3
- Ring = Finger #4
- Pinky = Finger #5

The finger numbers are the same for both hands. For example, the thumb is finger #1 in both the right hand and left hand and the pinky is finger #5 in both hands.

For Video Lesson 1, go to www.steeplechasemusic.com.

4

Three-Note Exercises: Using the Right Hand ("RH")

- Try these exercises, which use the notes C, D, and E in the right hand ("RH").
- In your right hand, use Thumb for Middle C, use Pointer for D, and use Middle Finger for E.
- Take a look at the keyboard chart and photo below and practice each one 5-10 times.
- As an extra bonus, try saying the letter names aloud as you play each exercise.
  This will help you associate the note name with the key and finger number.

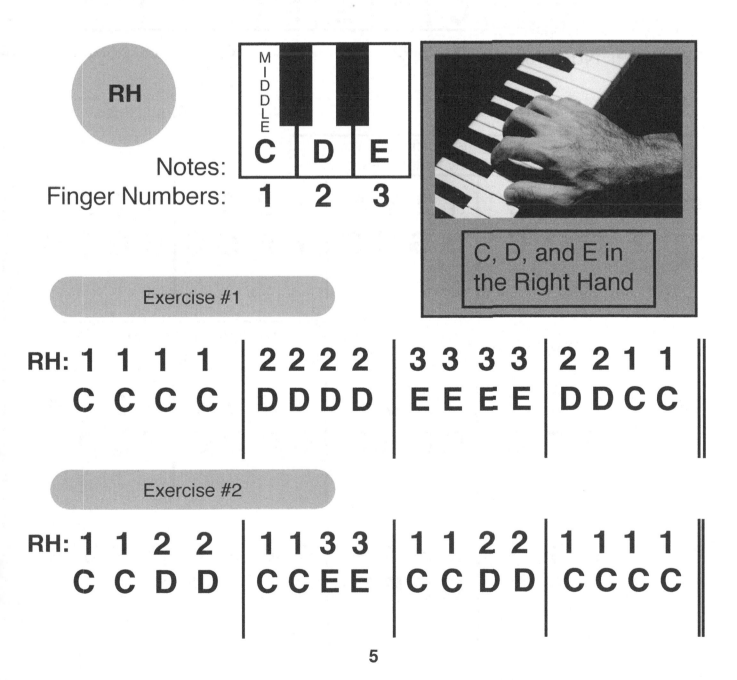

RH

Notes:
Finger Numbers:

MIDDLE C   D   E
1   2   3

C, D, and E in the Right Hand

Exercise #1

RH: 1 1 1 1 | 2 2 2 2 | 3 3 3 3 | 2 2 1 1 ‖
    C C C C | D D D D | E E E E | D D C C

Exercise #2

RH: 1 1 2 2 | 1 1 3 3 | 1 1 2 2 | 1 1 1 1 ‖
    C C D D | C C E E | C C D D | C C C C

5

Five-Note Pieces as Studies for the Right Hand (RH)

- Here are a few more pieces that use the five fingers of the right hand.
- Remember to find Middle C with the Thumb of your right hand (RH).

RH

Notes: C D E F G
Finger Numbers: 1 2 3 4 5

↑ ↑ — New Notes

Exercise #1

The numbers here are for <u>beats</u>, not fingers. When there is a blank space, don't play for that beat or beats.

Beats: 1 2 3 4 | 1 2 3 4 | 1 2 3 4 | 1 2 3 4
F E D C | G G G G | F E D C | G G C C

Ode to Joy

We will learn a more advanced version of Beethoven's *Ode to Joy,* later in this book.

Beats: 1 2 3 4 | 1 2 3 4 | 1 2 3 4 | 1 2 3 4
E E F G | G F E D | C C D E | E D D

Beats: 1 2 3 4 | 1 2 3 4 | 1 2 3 4 | 1 2 3 4
E E F G | G F E D | C C D E | D C C

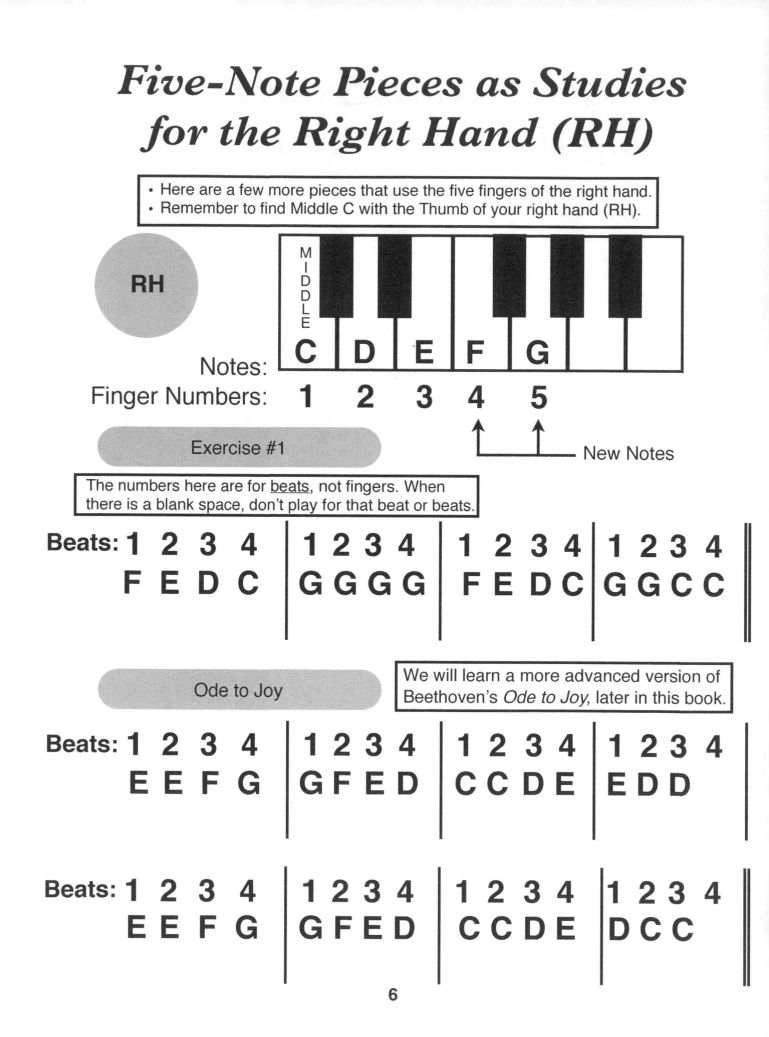

6

Three-Note Exercises: Studies for the Left Hand ("LH")

- Try these exercises, which use the notes A, B, and Middle C in the left hand ("LH").
- In your left hand, use Thumb for Middle C, use Pointer for B, and use Middle Finger for A.
- Take a look at the keyboard chart and photo below and practice each one 5-10 times.
- As an extra bonus, try saying the letter names aloud as you play each exercise.
  This will help you associate the note name with the key and finger number. *Have Fun!*

LH

Notes: | A | B | C (MIDDLE)

Finger Numbers: **3** **2** **1**

A, B, and C in the Left Hand

The numbers here are for <u>fingers</u>, not beats.

Exercise #1

LH: **1 1 2 3** | **1 1 2 3** | **2 2 3 3** | **2 2 3 3** ‖
C C B A | **C C B A** | **B B A A** | **B B A A**

Exercise #2

LH: **3 2 1 2** | **3 2 1 2** | **1 1 3 3** | **1 2 3 3** ‖
A B C B | **A B C B** | **C C A A** | **C B A A**

7

An Overview of Time Signatures

- Measures are composed of groups of beats called Time Signatures or Meter (both terms mean the same thing and are interchangeable).
- The most common Time Signatures (or "meters") are groups of 2, 3, or 4 beats per measure: 2/4, 3/4, and 4/4 Time Signatures.
- 2/4 Time Signature groups the notes into measures of 2 beats. Count: "One, Two" for each measure.
- 3/4 Time Signature groups the notes into measures of 3 beats. Count: "One, Two, Three" for each measure.
- 4/4 Time Signature groups the notes into measures of 4 beats. Count: "One, Two, Three, Four" for each measure.
- Below, are examples of sets of 4 measures in 2/4, 3/4, and 4/4.
- Count aloud and clap on the first beat for the exercises below.

Check out video 3

Example 1: 2/4 Time Signature
Try Clapping on the X: On the First Beat.

Example 2: 3/4 Time Signature
Try Clapping on the X: On the First Beat.

Example 3: 4/4 Time Signature
Try Clapping on the X: On the First Beat.

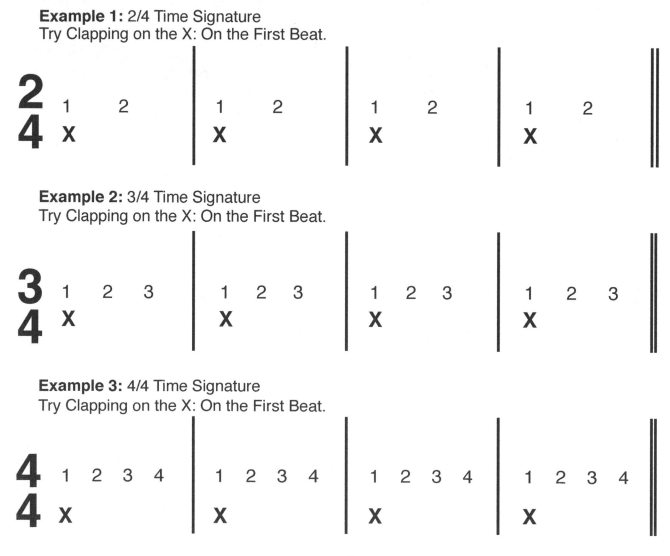

8

Putting Both Hands Together Using the Keyboard Notes: A,B,C,D & E

- Here are 2 pieces for both hands. They use the notes A, B, C, D, and E.
- The numbers listed are for the <u>beats</u>, not the finger numbers.
- If there is a blank space, don't play for that beat or beats.
- Both Thumbs will share Middle C.

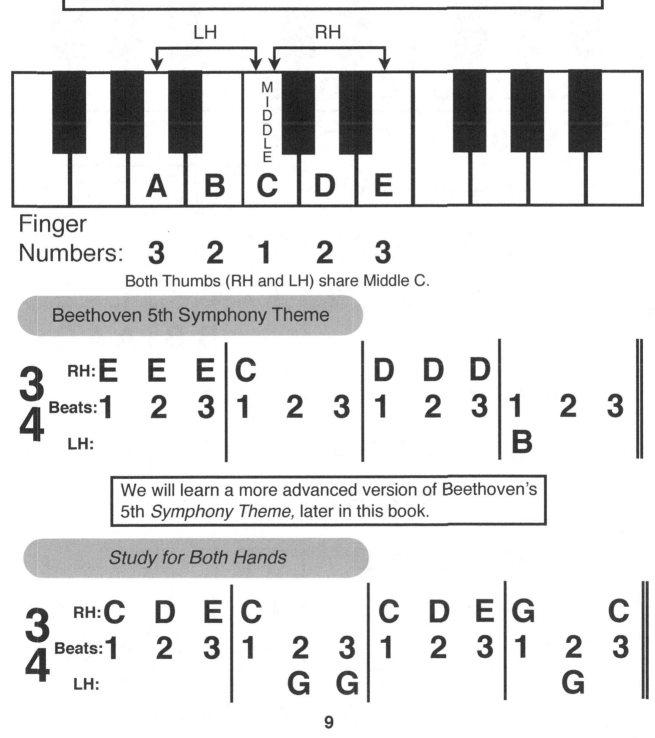

LH   RH

A B C D E

MIDDLE C

Finger Numbers: 3   2   1   2   3

Both Thumbs (RH and LH) share Middle C.

Beethoven 5th Symphony Theme

$\frac{3}{4}$

RH:	E	E	E	C			D	D	D	B		
Beats:	1	2	3	1	2	3	1	2	3	1	2	3
LH:										B		

We will learn a more advanced version of Beethoven's 5th *Symphony Theme,* later in this book.

Study for Both Hands

$\frac{3}{4}$

RH:	C	D	E	C			C	D	E	G		C
Beats:	1	2	3	1	2	3	1	2	3	1	2	3
LH:				G	G					G		

9

Mozart's Twinkle, Twinkle, Little Star with Both Hands: G,A,B,C,D,E & F

- If you see a blank space, don't play for that beat or beats.
- Remember to place both of your thumbs on Middle C.

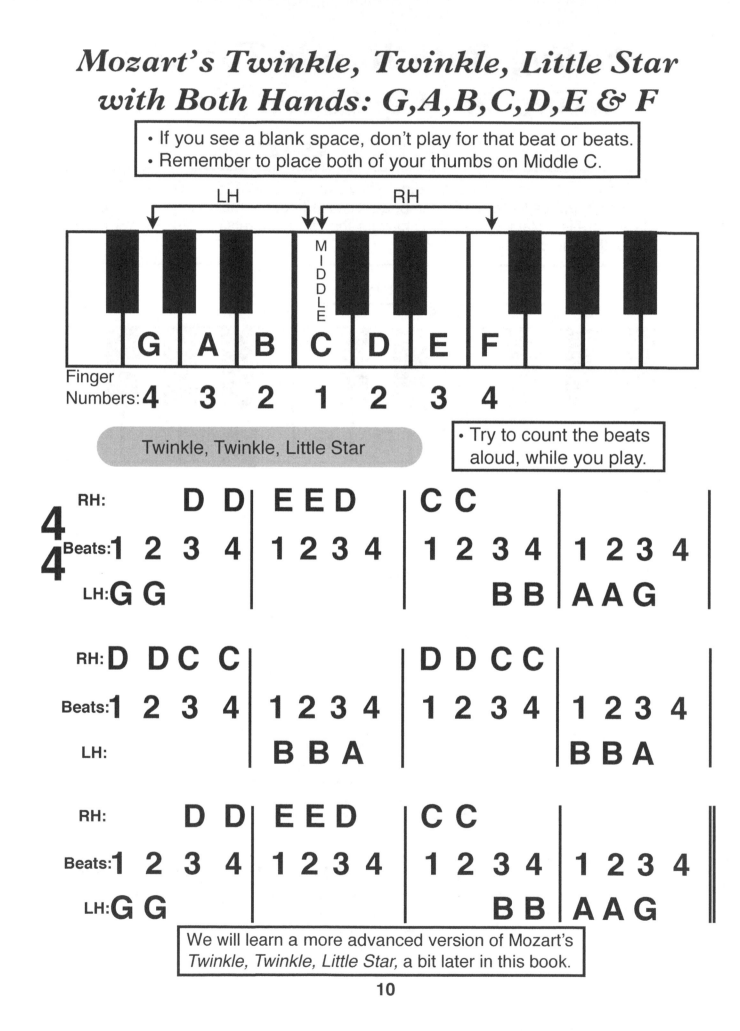

LH   RH

MIDDLE

| G | A | B | C | D | E | F |

Finger Numbers: 4 3 2 1 2 3 4

Twinkle, Twinkle, Little Star

- Try to count the beats aloud, while you play.

4/4

RH: D D | E E D | C C |
Beats: 1 2 3 4 | 1 2 3 4 | 1 2 3 4 | 1 2 3 4
LH: G G | | B B | A A G

RH: D D C C | | D D C C |
Beats: 1 2 3 4 | 1 2 3 4 | 1 2 3 4 | 1 2 3 4
LH: | B B A | | B B A

RH: D D | E E D | C C |
Beats: 1 2 3 4 | 1 2 3 4 | 1 2 3 4 | 1 2 3 4
LH: G G | | B B | A A G

We will learn a more advanced version of Mozart's *Twinkle, Twinkle, Little Star*, a bit later in this book.

10

Music Theory:
An Overview of Intervals

- In music, the distance between any 2 notes is called an "Interval".
- Intervals can be played at the same time, for example, if you press down two piano keys or they can be played one after the other, for example, if you play the note "C" and then the note "D".
- On the piano, the easiest way to understand intervals is to look at the keyboard. Play Middle C with your Left-Hand Index Finger, then play D with your Right-Hand Index finger. This interval is called a 2nd.
- Next, play Middle C with your Left-Hand Index Finger, then play E with your Right-Hand Index finger. This interval is called a 3rd.
- Follow these steps in the 2 diagrams below. Use the Left-Hand Index Finger when you see LH and use the Right-Hand Index Finger when you see RH.

Check out video 4

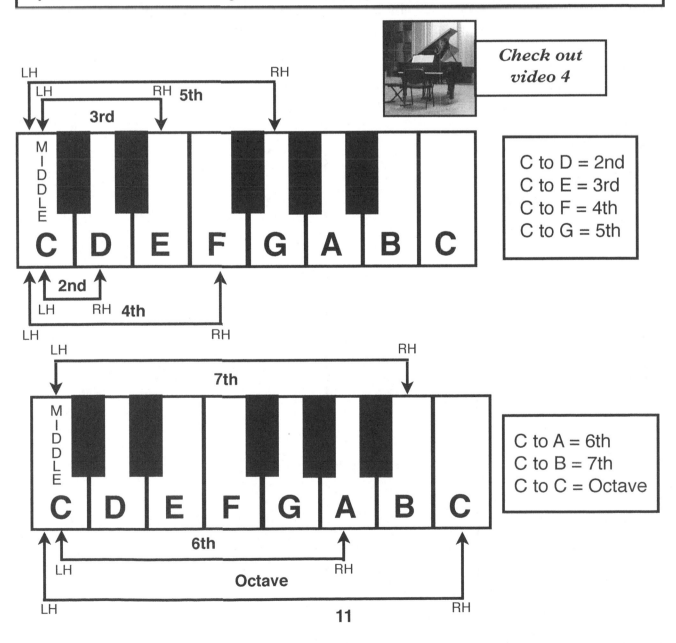

C to D = 2nd
C to E = 3rd
C to F = 4th
C to G = 5th

C to A = 6th
C to B = 7th
C to C = Octave

Basic Rhythms: Whole Notes, Half Notes & Quarter Notes

- Let's take a look at some basic rhythms.
- Quarter Notes are notes that get 1 Beat (or Count).
- Half Notes are notes that get 2 Beats (or Counts).
- Whole Notes are notes that get 4 Beats (or Counts).
- In the next 3 examples, try counting on each beat of the 4/4 measures aloud, for example: 1,2,3,4.
- Clap on the quarter, half, and whole notes.

Check out video 5

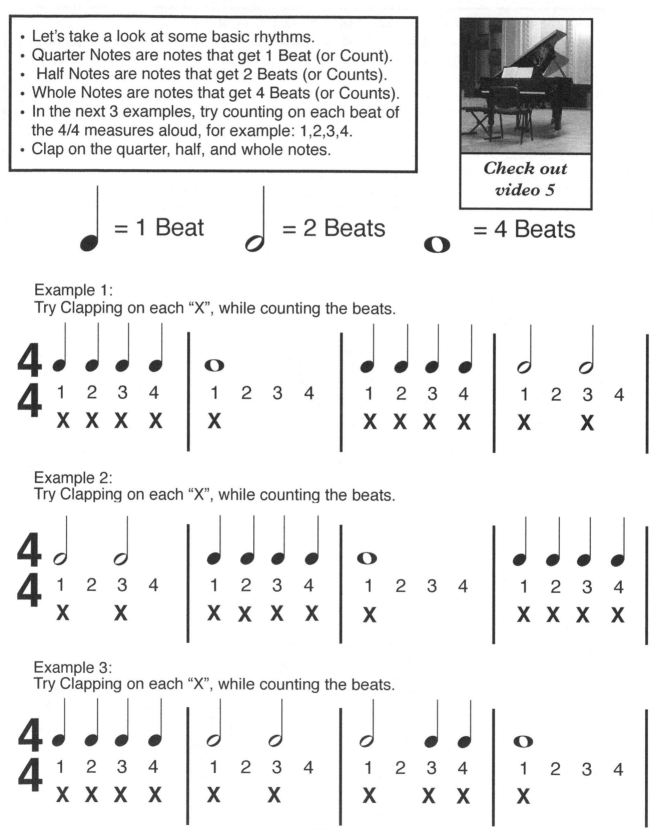

♩ = 1 Beat   ♪ = 2 Beats   𝅝 = 4 Beats

Example 1:
Try Clapping on each "X", while counting the beats.

Example 2:
Try Clapping on each "X", while counting the beats.

Example 3:
Try Clapping on each "X", while counting the beats.

12

Treble Clef Notes: Middle C, D & E

- The Treble Clef mainly is used for notes above Middle C.
- About 90% of the time, it is used for the Right Hand.
  (There are a few occasions in songs or pieces when it is used for the Left Hand.)
- The Treble Clef is made up of Lines and Spaces that correspond to keys on the piano.
  Each Line or Space is linked to <u>one</u> (and only one) key on the piano.
- We will learn more about the lines and spaces of the Treble Clef in the following lessons.

Middle C

Middle C is under the Treble Clef. There is a line through the middle of the note.

This is the TrebleClef Symbol:

Note:

Finger Number: **1**

MIDDLE **C**

RH

D

D is under the Treble Clef, as well. It hangs under the lowest line of the Treble Clef.

Check out video 6

Note:

Finger Number: **2**

D

RH

E

E is on the first line of the Treble Clef.

Note:

Finger Number: **3**

E

RH

13

Treble Clef Exercises: Middle C, D & E (RH)

- Let's play 4 exercises with notes of the Treble Clef: C, D, and E.
- Remember to find Middle C with the Thumb of your right hand (RH).

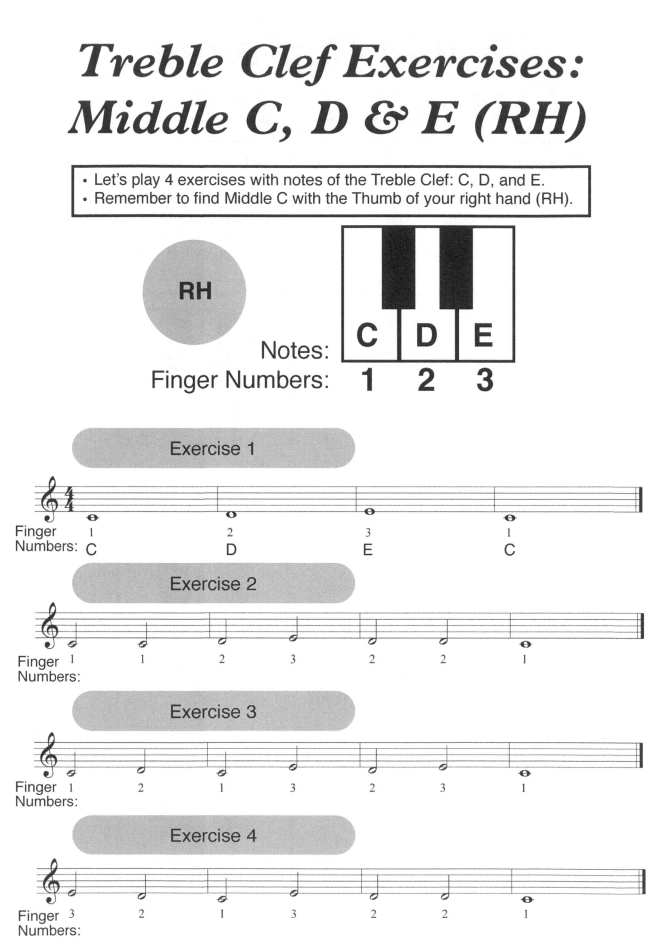

RH

Notes: C D E
Finger Numbers: 1 2 3

Exercise 1

Finger Numbers: 1 2 3 1
C D E C

Exercise 2

Finger Numbers: 1 1 2 3 2 2 1

Exercise 3

Finger Numbers: 1 2 1 3 2 3 1

Exercise 4

Finger Numbers: 3 2 1 3 2 2 1

14

More Treble Clef Exercises: Middle C, D, E & F (RH)

- Let's add the note F, which is on the 1st space of the Treble Clef.
- Remember to find Middle C with the Thumb of your right hand (RH).

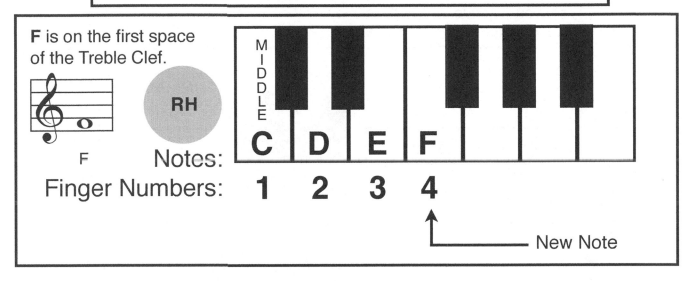

F is on the first space of the Treble Clef.

F

RH

Notes: C D E F

Finger Numbers: 1 2 3 4

New Note

Exercise 1

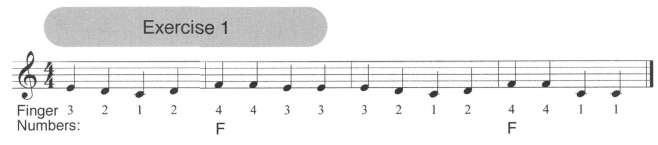

Finger Numbers: 3 2 1 2 — 4 4 3 3 — 3 2 1 2 — 4 4 1 1

F   F

Exercise 2

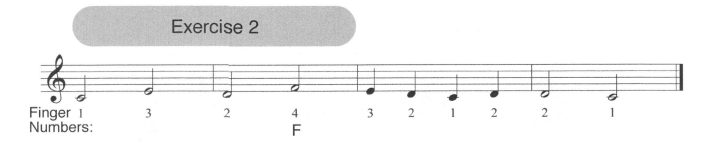

Finger Numbers: 1 3 2 4 — 3 2 1 2 — 2 1

F

Exercise 3

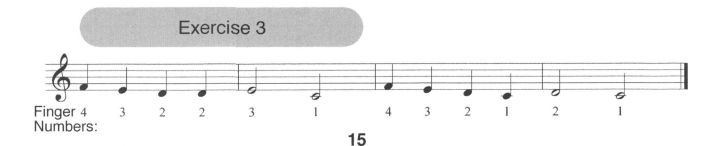

Finger Numbers: 4 3 2 2 3 1 — 4 3 2 1 2 1

15

Treble Clef Lines: Overview

- Each line of the Treble Clef stands for a specific note and key on the piano.
- The lines have numbers that go from 1 to 5. Line 1 is the lowest line. Line 5 is the top line (or highest line) on the Treble Clef.
- To help you remember the note names of each line, memorize the saying below. In the saying ("Every Good Bird Does Fly"). "Every" stands for "E", "Good" stands for "G", "Bird" stands for "B", "Does" stands for "D", and "Fly" stands for "F".
- The "E" of "Every" stands for the "E" piano key 2 notes above Middle C. See the charts below to better understand these notes.

Check out video 6

From bottom to top, this is the pattern for the lines: E, G, B, D, F

Line Numbers

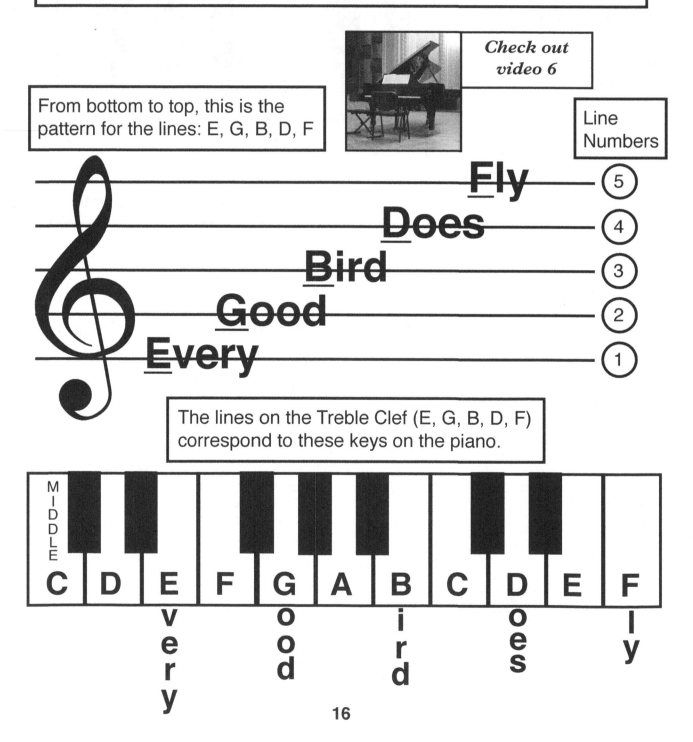

Fly — (5)
Does — (4)
Bird — (3)
Good — (2)
Every — (1)

The lines on the Treble Clef (E, G, B, D, F) correspond to these keys on the piano.

MIDDLE C | D | E (very) | F | G (good) | A | B (bird) | C | D (oes) | E | F (ly)

16

Treble Clef Spaces: Overview

- Each space of the Treble Clef stands for a specific note and key on the piano.
- The spaces have numbers that go from 1 to 4. Space 1 is the lowest space. Space 4 is the top space (or highest space) on the Treble Clef.
- To help you learn the note names of each space, remember that the spaces of the Treble Clef form the word "Face" spelled upside down (from bottom space to top.)
- The "F" of "Face" stands for the "F" piano key 4 notes above Middle C.
- See the charts below to better understand the other notes.

Check out video 6

From bottom to top, this is the pattern for the Spaces: F, A, C, E

Space Numbers

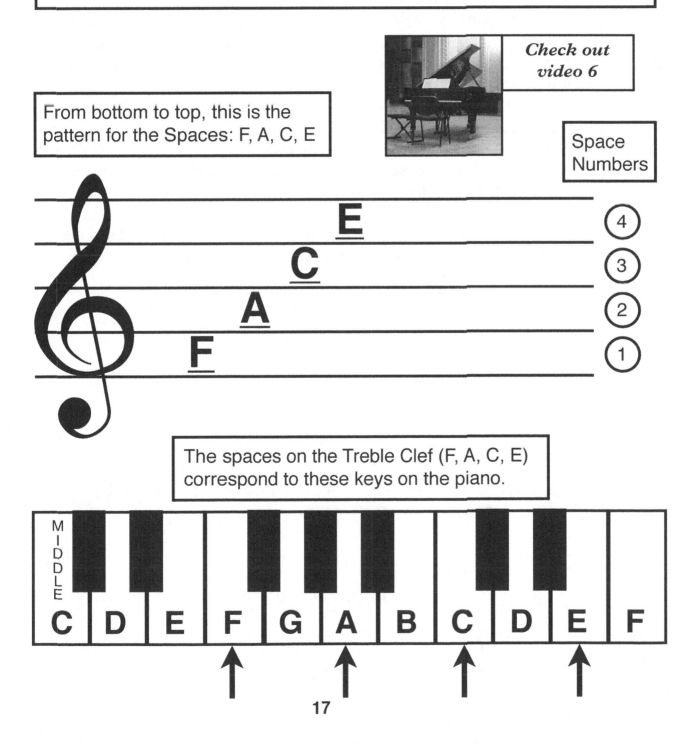

The spaces on the Treble Clef (F, A, C, E) correspond to these keys on the piano.

17

Tchaikovsky's Swan Lake Theme & Rossini's William Tell Overture Theme for the Right Hand

Let's take a look at the theme from Tchaikovsky's *Swan Lake*. This melody will be in the right hand. There will be two hand positions for the piece. The first hand position will cover the notes A, B, C, D, and E. For this position, place your thumb on the note A, which is six keys above middle C. The second position will cover the notes F, G, A, B, and C. For the second position, place your thumb on the note F, which is four keys above middle C.

For Rossini's *William Tell Overture*, which you might recognize as the theme from the *Lone Ranger*, the right hand will be on these notes G, B, C, D, and E. Place your thumb on the note G, five keys above middle C. There will be one key (the note A) between your thumb and index finger. We will present more advanced versions of each of these pieces later in the book.

The small numbers above the notes indicate the finger numbers. The brackets indicate the hand positions. The numbers below are for the beats. The letters for each note are indicated inside each note head. As you are playing, try to memorize the notes on the staff and make a connection with the piano keys.

Remember, you can download the free, MP3 audio files for all of the pieces in this book from the Steeplechase Music website. This way, you can hear how each piece sounds.

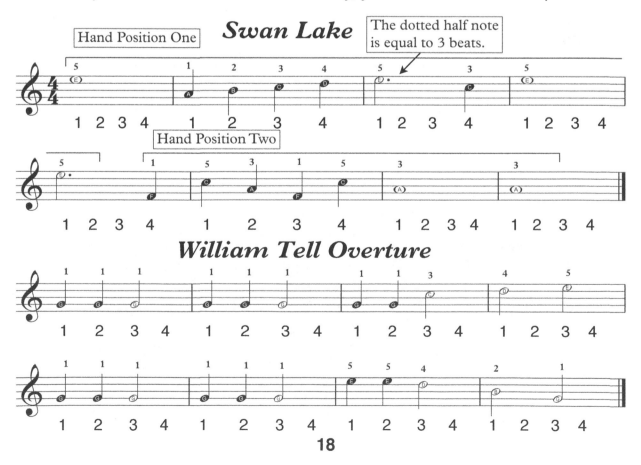

18

Bass Clef Notes: Middle C, B & A

- The Bass Clef mainly is used for notes below Middle C.
- About 90% of the time, it is used for the Left Hand.
  (There are a few occasions in pieces when it is used for the Right Hand.)
- The word "Bass" is pronounced like the word "Base" (as in "Baseball").
- The Bass Clef is made up of Lines and Spaces that correspond to keys on the piano.
  Each Line or Space is linked to <u>one</u> (and only one) key on the piano.
- We will learn more about the lines and spaces of the Bass Clef in the following lessons.

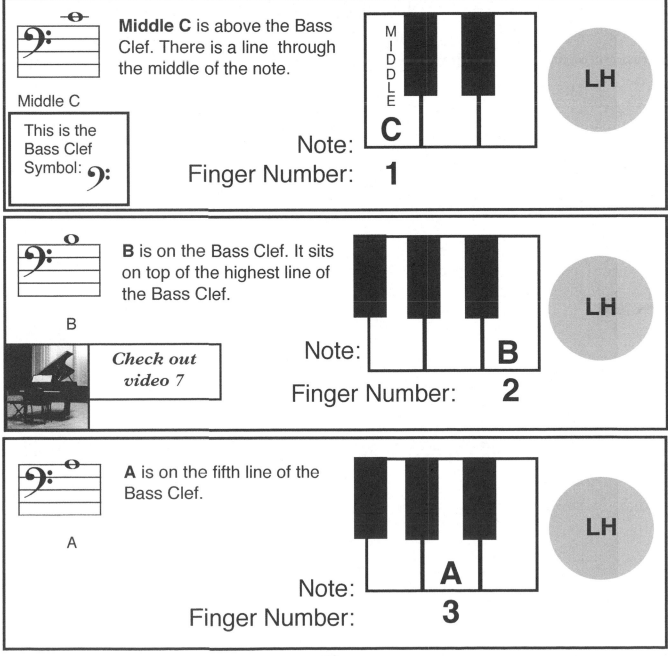

Middle C is above the Bass Clef. There is a line through the middle of the note.

Middle C

This is the Bass Clef Symbol: 𝄢

Note: C
Finger Number: **1**

B is on the Bass Clef. It sits on top of the highest line of the Bass Clef.

B

Check out video 7

Note: B
Finger Number: **2**

A is on the fifth line of the Bass Clef.

A

Note: A
Finger Number: **3**

19

Bass Clef Exercises: A, B & Middle C

- Let's play 4 exercises with notes of the Bass Clef: A, B, and C.
- Remember to find Middle C with the Thumb of your left hand (LH).

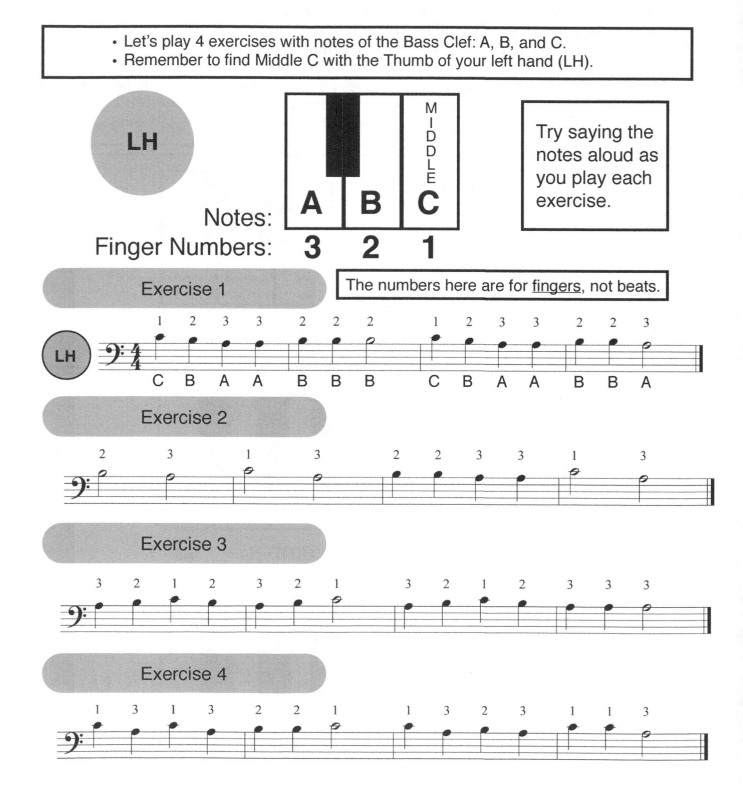

LH

Notes: A B C (MIDDLE)

Finger Numbers: 3 2 1

Try saying the notes aloud as you play each exercise.

Exercise 1

The numbers here are for <u>fingers</u>, not beats.

1 2 3 3 2 2 2 1 2 3 3 2 2 3
C B A A B B B C B A A B B A

Exercise 2

2 3 1 3 2 2 3 3 1 3

Exercise 3

3 2 1 2 3 2 1 3 2 1 2 3 3 3

Exercise 4

1 3 1 3 2 2 1 1 3 2 3 1 1 3

20

Bass Clef Lines: Overview

- Each line of the Bass Clef stands for a specific note and key on the piano.
- The lines have numbers that go from 1 to 5. Line 1 is the lowest line. Line 5 is the top line (or highest line) on the Bass Clef.
- To help you remember the note names of each line, memorize the saying below. In the saying ("Good Baked Desserts For All"). "Good" stands for "G", "Baked" stands for "B", "Desserts" stands for "D", "For" stands for "F", and "All" stands for "A".
- The "A" of "All" stands for the "A" piano key two notes below Middle C. See the charts below to better understand these notes.

Check out video 7

From bottom to top, this is the pattern for the lines: G, B, D, F, A

Line Numbers

All — 5
For — 4
Desserts — 3
Baked — 2
Good — 1

The lines on the Bass Clef (G, B, D, F, A) correspond to these keys on the piano.

F G A B C D E F G A B C (MIDDLE)

Good Baked Desserts For All

21

Bass Clef Spaces: Overview

- Each space of the Bass Clef stands for a specific note and key on the piano.
- The spaces have numbers that go from 1 to 4. Space 1 is the lowest space. Space 4 is the top space (or highest space) on the Bass Clef.
- To help you learn the note names of each space, remember that the spaces of the Bass Clef form the phrase "All cows eat grass".
- The word "All" stands for the key and note "A"; the word "Cows" stands for "C".
- See the charts below to better understand the other notes.

Check out video 7

Space Numbers

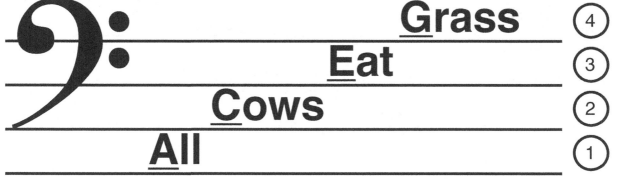

	Space Numbers
Grass	4
Eat	3
Cows	2
All	1

The spaces on the Bass Clef (A, C, E, G) correspond to these keys on the piano.

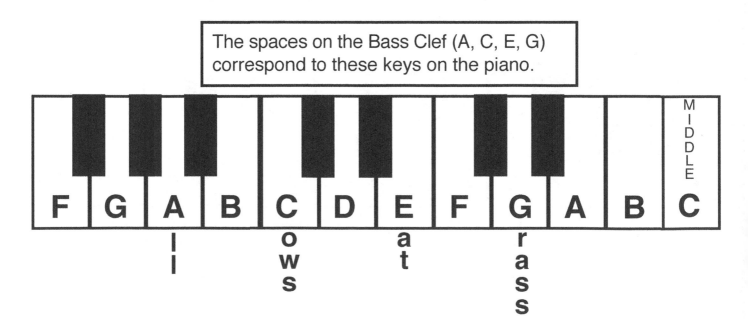

F	G	A	B	C	D	E	F	G	A	B	C
		l l		o w s		a t		r a s s			MIDDLE

22

Grieg's Hall of the Mountain King & Pachelbel's Canon: For the Left Hand

These next two pieces are studies for the left hand.

For Grieg's *Hall of the Mountain King*, start with the fifth finger (pinky) of your left hand on the key of D, which is seven keys below middle C. The notes for hand position one are D, E, F, G and A. In measure six of the piece, you will shift your hand position and play the A with the third finger (middle finger) of your left hand. The notes for hand position two are F, A, middle C and D.

For Pachelbel's *Canon*, there are four easy left-hand positions. Each hand position uses only three fingers: thumb, index, and middle finger. You will start on middle C for hand position one. For hand position two, you will move your thumb to G (the top space of the bass clef). In hand position three, you will move your thumb to E (just two notes above middle C). Place your thumb on B (just below middle C) for hand position number four. For the last note of the piece (C), just move your thumb one key higher than B (to middle C).

Remember, you can download the free, MP3 audio files for all of the pieces in this book from the Steeplechase Music website. This way, you can hear how each piece sounds.

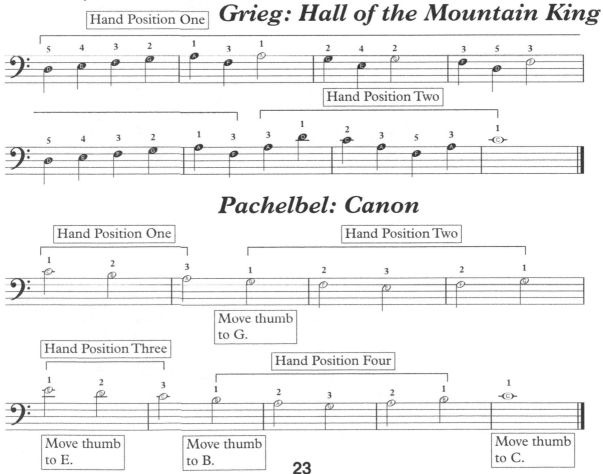

Grieg: Hall of the Mountain King

Pachelbel: Canon

23

Easy Left-Hand Chords: C Major, F Major & G7

- Chords are 3 or more notes played at the same time.
- In order to play chords well, keep your fingers curved for the notes that you play and lift your fingers that are not being used for the chord.
- Take a look at video lesson 8 to see and hear how these techniques work.
- For these chords, use the Left Hand (LH).
- We are going to look at 3 chords in this lesson.

See Video Lesson 8

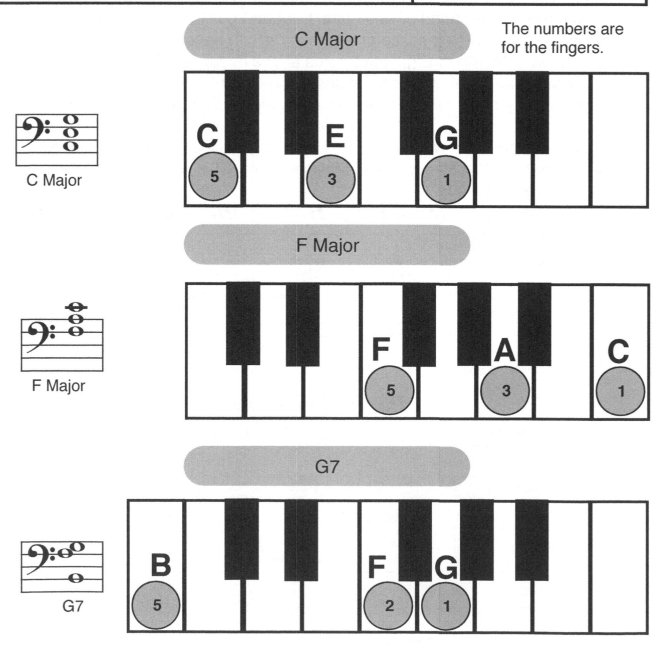

More Easy Left-Hand Chords
A Minor, D Minor & G Major

- Let's look at 3 more chords for the Left Hand: A Minor, D Minor, & G Major.
- Make sure to keep your fingers curved and lift the fingers that do not play.

Check out video 8

The numbers are for the fingers.

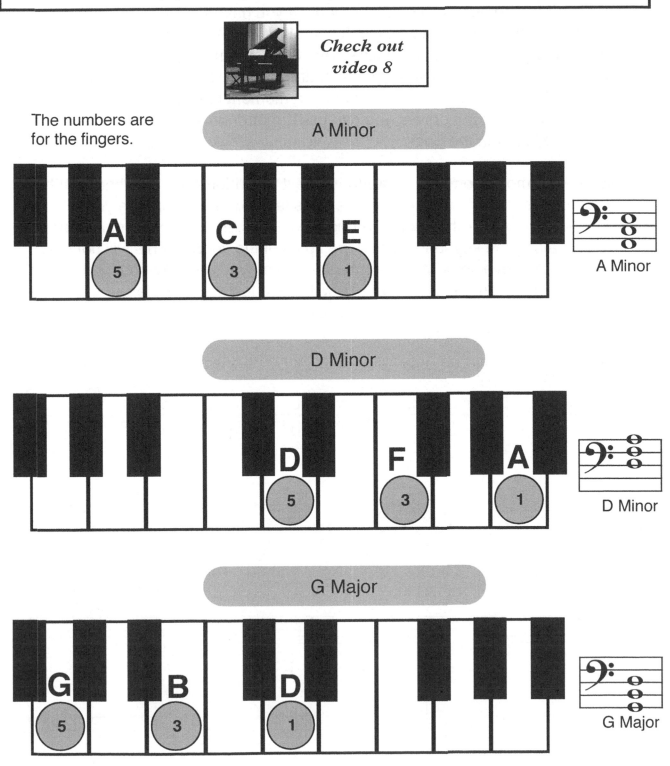

A Minor

A — 5   C — 3   E — 1

A Minor

D Minor

D — 5   F — 3   A — 1

D Minor

G Major

G — 5   B — 3   D — 1

G Major

25

Left-Hand Chord Studies

In this lesson, we are going to practice playing some of the chords from the previous two lessons. With each of these exercises, take your time to master the transition from one chord to the next. Building up this kind of left-hand coordination will greatly help you, once we start learning the pieces from the next section of the book. If you have a metronome, you might set it to quarter note equals 60 (in other words sixty beats per minute) for this exercise. As a side note, there are many free metronome apps available online. If you have a smart phone, tablet, computer, or similar electronic device, you might take a moment to find a free metronome app for it online; you can use a metronome to help you learn the pieces later in the book.

When you move from one chord to the next, try to form the new chord with your fingers, before playing the keys. This technique will improve your muscle memory for the chords. Along these lines, try to avoid sliding your fingers along the keyboard to find the notes of the chords. This will not only hamper the development of your muscle memory for playing chords, but it will also make it more likely that you will play a few wrong notes.

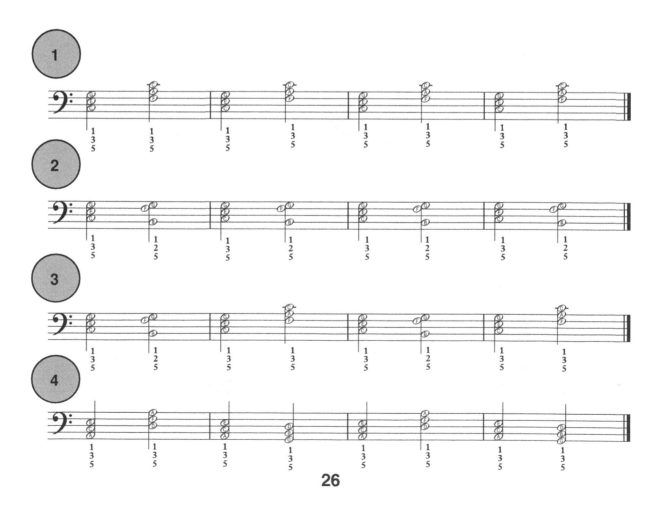

26

The Grand Staff: Overview

- The Grand Staff is formed by combining the Treble and Bass Clefs.
- All of the rules that we have learned so far about both clefs are still true for the Grand Staff. Using the Grand Staff makes it easier to read music written for both hands.
- Study the chart below to understand how the Staff works.

See Video Lesson 9

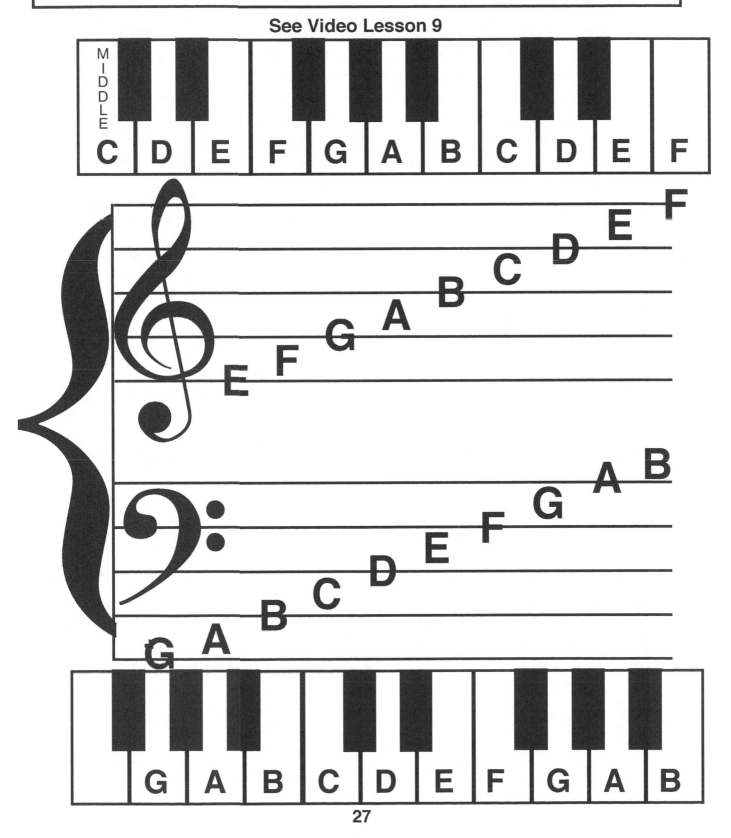

27

Naming the Notes on the Grand Staff

For this lesson, let's try naming the notes on the grand staff below. Remember to use your note-name sayings from earlier in the book. You may also refer back to the grand staff on the previous page. Try naming the notes for one measure, then go back and repeat naming the notes for that measure three times. Once you feel confident about the note names, go on to the next measure. After you have finished naming the notes on the entire page, go back to the beginning of the lesson and slowly play each note on the piano. You might also say the note aloud as you play it. This will begin to reinforce your understanding of the notes on the page and the keys on the piano keyboard.

28

Music Theory:
What are Sharps & Flats?

- On the piano, there are two types of keys: Black Keys and White Keys.
- The White Keys stand for natural notes, for example, C, D, E, F, G, A and B.
- The Black Keys (also called "accidentals") stand for Sharp or Flat Notes.
- Sharp Notes use this symbol: #
- Flat Notes use this symbol: ♭
- Here are some examples of Sharp Notes: F#, G#, A#, C#, D#
- Here are some examples of Flat Notes: Gb, Ab, Bb, Db, Eb

- On the piano keyboard, Sharp Keys are located directly to the right of their corresponding Natural Key (White Key). For example, F Sharp (F#) is the next key to the right from F (also called "F Natural"). C Sharp (C#) is the black key directly to the right of C (also called "C Natural").
- This pattern, of going to the next key directly to the right, holds true for all of the sharp notes going up and down the piano keyboard.
- Using the chart below, try locating the following sharp keys on the piano: C#, F#, D#, A#, G#.

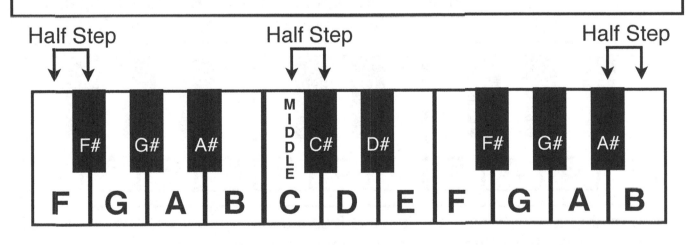

- The distance from a White Key to a Black Key, for example, F to F#, C to C#, or A# to B, is called a **Half Step** or Minor Second. **Remember this.** It is a bit of important information we will be referring to many times in the next book.

Music Theory: More on Sharps and Flats

- On the piano keyboard, Flat Keys are located directly to the left of their corresponding Natural Key (White Key). For example, G Flat (Gb) is the next black key to the left from G (also called "G Natural"). E Flat (Eb) is the black key directly to the left of E (also called "E Natural").
- This pattern, of going to the next key directly to the left, holds true for all of the flat notes going up and down the piano keyboard.
- Using the chart below, try locating the following flat keys on the piano: Ab, Db, Gb, Eb, Bb. **Remember: This pattern is the same for the entire keyboard.**

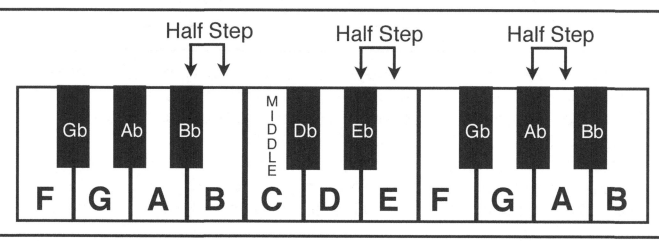

- The distance (up or down) from a White Key to a Black Key, for example, from B to Bb, Eb to E, or A to Ab, is called a Half Step or Minor Second. See Above.

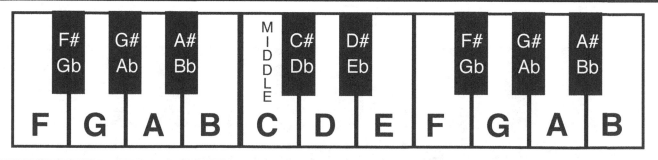

- You might have noticed in the last two lessons that there are 2 names for each Black Key: A Sharp Name and a Flat Name. This is true for the entire piano.
- Depending on the musical context (which we will learn more about throughout this book), a black key may be called by either its sharp or flat name. For example, A Flat and G Sharp are the same key on the piano; C Sharp and D Flat are the same key; and F Sharp and G Flat are the same key. See Above.

30

Scarborough Fair

- *Scarborough Fair* is in 3/4 time. Count: "One, Two, Three" for each measure.
- Place your left-hand thumb on middle C and your right-hand thumb on the D, which is located next to middle C on the right-hand side.
- For the F#, play the black key directly to the right of F on the piano.

Section 2: Famous Pieces by Great Composers

Throughout Section 2, we will go over strategies that will make learning each piece easier for you. As we get started with this section, I would like to mention one approach that will greatly aid in your learning these pieces:

Try this: Focus on learning only one or two measures at a time, starting with the right hand, then the left hand, and, finally, when you have mastered playing the music for each hand separately, play both hands together. Then, repeat this process for learning the next measure or two measures of the piece. This approach will greatly speed up your learning. It will also make your playing of the pieces much more secure. Please focus on this approach in your practice sessions, rather than only playing the piece from beginning to end.

Here are some of the concepts and techniques that you will learn, along with the pieces, in this section of the book:

- dynamics
- crescendo and diminuendo markings
- dotted eighth notes
- subdividing
- coordinating both hands
- counting beats
- reading in both clefs
- slurs: phase markers
- left-hand accompaniment styles
- upbeats
- thumb-under technique
- Alberti Bass
- ties

Remember, you can download and listen to a recording of all the pieces in the book by going to steeplechasemusic.com and downloading the free MP3 audio file from the book's webpage.

32

Beethoven's Ode to Joy: Overview on Dynamics

As our first piece, let's look at this easy, piano version of the famous theme from Beethoven's ninth symphony. The piece starts on the next page. Before we begin, let's look at a few music concepts that will help you play the piece.

Dynamics is a term that we use for the loudness and softness of the notes in music. In pieces and songs you will see dynamic indications represented as letters (F, P, MP, or MF, for example). These letters are abbreviations for Italian words.

p stands for the term "piano", which means soft (like a whisper, but not the quietest whisper).

mp stands for the term "mezzo-piano", which means medium soft (like a quiet conversation).

mf stands for the term "mezzo-forte", which means medium loud (like a normal conversation).

f stands for the term "forte", which means loud (like a shout).

Dynamics are a relative concept in music. In other words, you might consider that each piece has a slightly different range from soft to loud. Forte ("loud") in the context of a Beethoven piece may be a little different than forte in a Mozart piece. So, let's think of dynamics as a general concept that varies slightly from piece to piece. Part of what makes music so exciting and inspiring is finding the nuance and detail in the poetics of each piece. Exploring dynamics on the piano, along with many other musical concepts, will be a big part of this book.

In piano sheet music (sometimes called the "score"), we are given indications on how to make the music gradually louder or softer. In a lighthearted way, you might think of this as the piano version of turning up or turning down the volume on a car stereo, TV, or an audio device. In piano music we use two symbols:

Crescendo means to get gradually louder

Diminuendo means to get gradually quieter

Ode to Joy
(Theme from the 9th Symphony)

Make the right-hand melody a little louder than the left-hand chords for the piece.

Ludwig van Beethoven

The numbers below the notes are for the finger numbers.

The melody goes from the D (in the right hand) to the G (in the left hand). Follow the dashed arrow.

Make this section a little quieter. It starts mezzo-piano ("medium soft").

34

A Lesson on Mozart's Twinkle, Twinkle, Little Star:

Did you know that Mozart made twelve variations on the famous melody to *Twinkle, Twinkle, Little Star*? In this lesson, we are going to look at the left-hand chords for the piece and also practice playing right-hand staccato notes.

The names of the notes are indicated inside each note. The note names will be included for the pieces at the beginning of this part of the book. However, little by little, we are going to take the note names away. So, start to memorize the notes on the staff. Remember to use the sayings for the treble and bass clefs. You might also refer back to the treble and bass clef lessons from Section 1 of the book. For learning chords, name the notes from bottom to top.

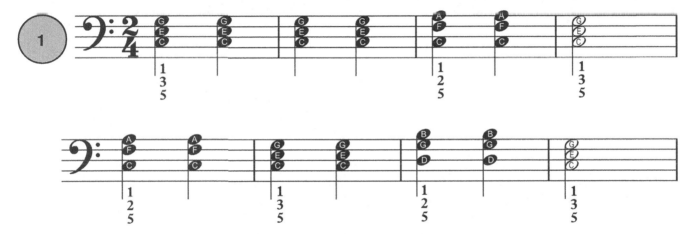

Let's look first at the left-hand chords, in exercise one. We have three chords for the left hand: C major, F major, and G major. The C major chord uses the notes C, E, and G (from bottom note to top). This F major chord uses the notes C, F, and A (from bottom to top). The G major chord we are using for the piece has the notes D, G, and B from bottom to top.

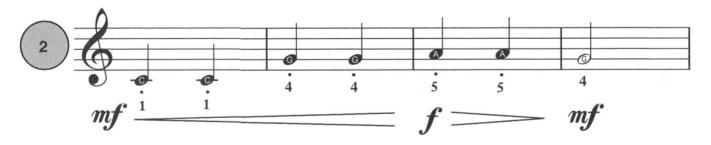

Next, in exercise two, let's practice the first part of the right-hand melody. There will be a little stretch between your right-hand thumb, when you go from C to G. Also, please note that there are staccato symbols (the dots below the notes) for the melody. These staccato symbols indicate that the notes should be played in a bouncy, disconnected manner. Have fun playing the pieces and try to make a lively sound for the melody.

35

Twinkle, Twinkle, Little Star

Wolfgang Amadeus Mozart

Play right hand alone, then left hand alone for each four-measure group. Then, put both hands together.

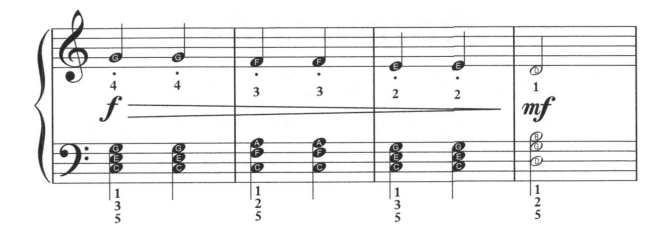

Listen for any patterns in the melody or chords that repeat other sections. Make a mental note of these repetitions. This will make it easier to play the entire piece. Try using this kind of technique for the other pieces in this book. Have fun!

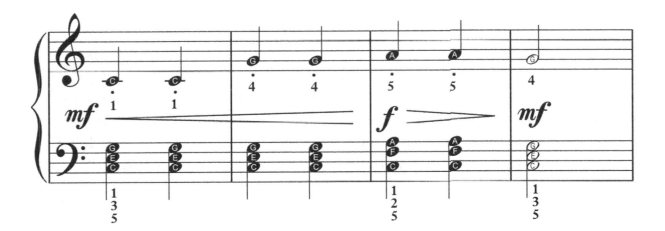

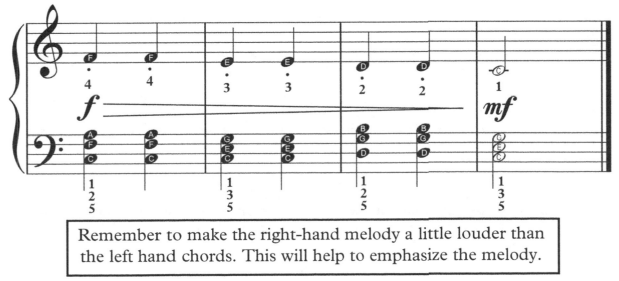

Remember to make the right-hand melody a little louder than the left hand chords. This will help to emphasize the melody.

Simple Gifts: Overview & Lesson

Simple Gifts is a wonderful Americana theme that inspired Aaron Copland in his famous piece, *Appalachian Spring*. The theme has a dancelike character, which is energized by the use of eighth notes in the melody. Eighth notes are equal to half of a quarter note and are counted as half of a beat.

They look like this:

In a measure of 4/4 time, eight eighth notes would be counted like this: 1 &, 2 &, 3 &, 4 &. The "&" stands for the word "and". The "&" or "and" is the halfway point of a beat. See the example below:

Musicians often refer the the halfway point of a beat as the "and". For example, a musician might say, "play it on the *and* of *two*". This would mean: play it at the halfway point between beats two and three. Try to find it in the above example.

When you divide a beat into sections, it is called "subdividing". Let's practice counting and playing groups of eighth notes and quarter notes. Use middle C. Remember to subdivide the eighth notes: for example, 1 &, 2 &, 3 &, 4 &.

38

In exercise one, we discover that the melody is exchanged between the left and right hands. The melody starts in the left hand and then moves to the right hand. Also, the first note is an upbeat or pickup note. This is a device that helps emphasize part of a musical phrase. The first note (G) leans into the second note (middle C). The G will be on the fourth beat of the measure. Count: 1, 2, 3, 4. On beat four, play the G. Then go into the next measure, the first full measure, and play middle C on the downbeat (beat one).

In piano music, phrases (the musical equivalent of sentences in language) are indicated by the use of slurs (or phrase markers). Slurs are curved lines that go over or under two or more different notes. When you finish a phrase in music, you should lift your hand or fingers a little bit to separate it from the next phrase. Slurs also indicate to play in a smooth (*legato*) manner on the piano. You can see some slurs in the piece's melody.

Let's now practice the melody in the left hand, as exercise two. Start this exercise slowly and then gradually build up the speed. Make sure that you pay special attention to the finger numbers; there are a few little shifts.

Simple Gifts

Remember to subdivide
for the eighth notes.

Practice the left-hand
chords alone, until they
are comfortable, before
playing with both hands.

The note names are
listed inside each note.

The dynamic marks indicate how
loud or soft to play the piece. They
also indicate whether the music
should get gradually louder or softer.

40

Practice the piece slowly, mastering one system (a line of music) at a time, before moving on to the next system. This way, you will learn the music faster, assembling and mastering one section of music, before moving on to the next.

The melody moves between hands here.

Practice the right-hand chords alone, until they are comfortable, before playing with both hands.

Pay attention to the finger numbers in the left hand.

41

Lesson on Brahms' Lullaby

Let's look at this famous lullaby by Johannes Brahms. In exercise one, we are going to focus on the left hand. This left-hand chord style of alternating a bass note with a small chord is a very common technique in piano playing. Some people refer to it as the "um, pa, pa" style, since it simulates the sound of an orchestra or band playing the accompaniment (or background music) for a melody. When playing this "um, pa, pa" style, lean your hand and wrist down slightly and to the left a little bit to emphasize the first note of the measure; in measure one, this would be the low note C. Then, slightly lift your hand back to its regular position for the second two beats; for the first measures, this would be the chords with the notes E and G. Follow this same motion for the entire piece. Count 1, 2, 3 for each measure.

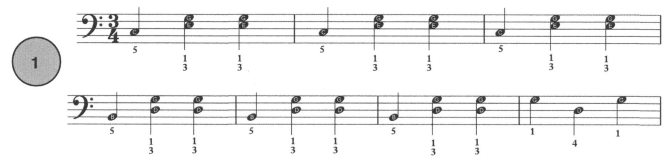

In exercise two, let's look at the beginning melody of the piece. The music is in 3/4 time signature. This means that there will be three beats in a measure and that the quarter note will get the beat. Also, the first measure is an upbeat. An upbeat is a note or set of notes that push into the downbeat (the first beat of the next measure). You might think of the phrase "the end", where the word "the" is accented to emphasize the word "end". Try saying it emphasizing the word "the": **The** end. A similar effect takes place for the two E notes that begin the melody. They are slightly accented to "push" into the G, which is the third note of the melody. Count: 1, 2, 3. On the count of three, play the upbeat E. This upbeat figure occurs several times in the lullaby. Once you start practicing the piece, listen for when it happens. We will hear and see upbeat figures in many of the pieces later in this book.

For exercise three, let's put both hands together. Try this slowly and then gradually build up the speed to a moderate tempo. Remember to count to three (1,2, 3) for each measure. Also, remember the upbeat figure at the beginning.

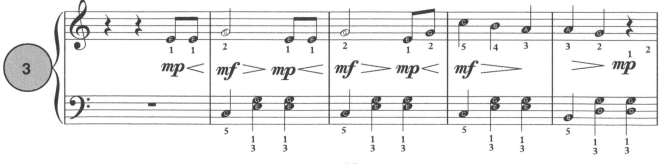

42

Lullaby

♩ = 72 — For each measure count 1, 2, 3.

Johannes Brahms

Remember, you can download and listen to a recording of all the pieces in the book by going to steeplechasemusic.com and downloading the free MP3 audio file from the book's webpage.

43

Haydn's Surprise Symphony: Overview

In exercise one, let's practice the opening measures of Haydn's *Surprise Symphony* theme. Starting on middle C, this first part fits comfortably under the right hand with one finger per key.

Check out video 10

Exercise two features the left hand. In measure 3, you have two versions of a G major chord. Practice finding these chords and moving from one chord to the next.

Now, in exercise three, let's put exercises one and two together. Take your time and practice each measure slowly. Then, gradually speed up to a moderate tempo.

Exercise four is for the left hand. In measure three, you will shift your hand position by moving your thumb up to middle C. In measure three, there is also a sharp note. To play this F# move your fourth finger (ring finger) up to the black key directly to the right of F. This F# will carry over to the F (the next note in the measure) and make it an F#.

Move your thumb up to middle C.

Exercise five is for the right hand and starts with the thumb one octave (eight notes) above middle C. In measure three, you will move your 5th finger up to the C that is two octaves above middle C.

The F# is carried over.

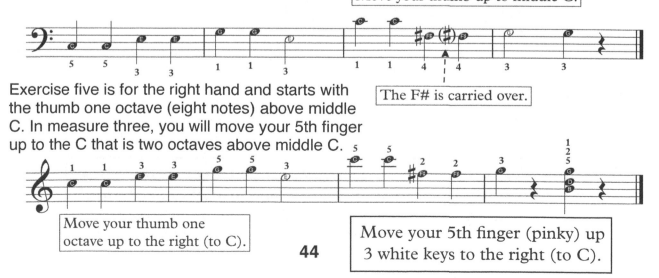

Move your thumb one octave up to the right (to C).

Move your 5th finger (pinky) up 3 white keys to the right (to C).

44

Surprise Symphony Theme

Joseph Haydn

The F# carries over.

Bring out the left hand here.

Move your thumb one octave up to the right (to C)

Move your 5th finger up to C.

Move your 5th finger one key up to the right (to D)

45

Lesson on Dvořák's
New World Symphony Theme & Dotted Rhythms

In Dvořák's *Theme from the New World Symphony,* we have a few interesting musical concepts. The first one is syncopation. Syncopation is when notes occur on weaker beats or between beats. The strongest beat in every measure is beat 1, which is called the "downbeat" of the measure. In 4/4 time, beat 3 is the second strongest beat.

When notes occur between beats, we have to use a technique called subdividing to count the rhythm. We talked about subdividing for our lesson on *Simple Gifts,* as well. Subdividing means that we are going to cut the beats into smaller sections. The simplest of these subdivisions is to cut each beat in half. In music, we use the word "and" and the symbol "&" for the halfway point between each beat. For example, if we have a measure of 4/4 time, where we want to subdivide each beat in half we would count: "1 & 2 & 3 & 4 &". Try counting it aloud. The eighth notes (notes with a flag or beam), count as half of a beat. In other words, two eighth notes equal one quarter note.

Just to refresh your memory, this is what an eighth note looks like: ♪

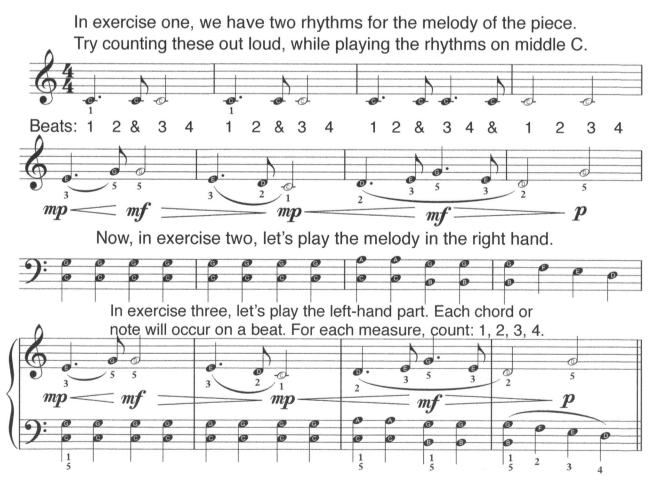

In exercise one, we have two rhythms for the melody of the piece. Try counting these out loud, while playing the rhythms on middle C.

Beats: 1 2 & 3 4   1 2 & 3 4   1 2 & 3 4 & 1 2 3 4

Now, in exercise two, let's play the melody in the right hand.

In exercise three, let's play the left-hand part. Each chord or note will occur on a beat. For each measure, count: 1, 2, 3, 4.

Now, let's put both hands together for exercise four. Listen to how the right hand is syncopated against the left hand. Remember to subdivide while you are counting.

Play hands alone for the whole piece first, then, one system at a time, add both hands.

New World Symphony Theme

Antonín Dvořák

The comma means lift your hand to separate the notes.

For the next two lines, move your right-hand thumb up to F (four notes to the right).

8va means to play one octave (eight notes) higher than written.

Bring out the melody in the left hand.

47

Joy to the World Overview & Lesson

With *Joy to the World*, we are going to learn a new and very useful piano concept: moving the right-hand thumb under and third finger over. This technique will allow us to smoothly connect different finger positions on the piano. In this progression of exercises, we will practice the technique, which is used in *Joy to the World* and many other pieces.

Use these notes for the first hand position in the right hand.

In exercise one, let's practice the first right-hand position: F, G, A, B, C.

Check out video 11

Use these notes for the second hand position in the right hand.

In exercise two, let's practice the second right-hand position: C, D, E, F, G.

Use these notes for the first hand position in the right hand.

Third finger goes over the to thumb for the second, right-hand position.

Now, let's go back to position one and shift into position two by moving the third finger over the thumb (from F to E) in measure 4. You may start to hear a little bit of the tune. This is the "finger-over" technique. We will use it many times in the upcoming pieces.

Joy   to   the   world____   the   Lord   is   born.

In exercise four, let's now add the melody with the correct rhythm.

For exercise five, let's practice the chords for the left hand.

Use first hand position.

Third finger over to second hand position.

Now, for exercise six, let's put both hands together.

48

Joy to the World

Use first hand position.

Third finger over to second hand position.

George Frideric Handel

Go back to the first hand position.

Third finger over.

Go back to the first hand position.

Go to second hand position.

Go to first hand position.

Go to second hand position.

Third finger over.

49

Lesson on Brahms' Hungarian Dance, Alberti Bass & Ties

Brahms' *Hungarian Dance* features a very important left-hand accompaniment figure, which is called "Alberti Bass". As a common, left-hand technique in piano music, Alberti Bass provides harmonic and rhythmic energy and movement for a piece. The way it works is that instead of playing all the notes of a chord at the same time in the left hand, you will play the notes of the chord one at a time, in an alternating pattern.

If you look at exercise one, the first two measures contain an A minor chord (the notes A, C & E). Instead of playing all three notes at the same time, we are going to play one note at a time going from fifth finger (pinky) to first finger (thumb) to third finger (middle) and finally back to first finger (thumb). This will make a propulsive, rocking sound for the left hand. In measure three, as the chords change, the Alberti Bass gives a little extra harmonic excitement to the music. Let's give exercise one a try.

In exercise two, we are going to look at another important music concept: ties. Ties are curved lines that connect two of the same notes so that their duration is combined. In other words, if you tie a whole note D (four beats) to a half note D (two beats), you would hold down the key for D for six beats (four beats plus two beats). It would look like this:

Ties are curved lines that connect two of the same notes (like two Es or two Ds). The notes that are tied must be next to each other. Ties can connect two notes in the same measure or they can connect two notes from different measures. They always, only connect the **same** notes (like two Gs). You will **never** see a tie connecting two different notes (like a tie from a C to a G). The curved lines of ties can go over or under these two notes; whether the tie (the curved line) is above or below the notes really depends on the page layout for the music, nothing more. In other words, it does not mean anything different if the tie is above or below the notes.

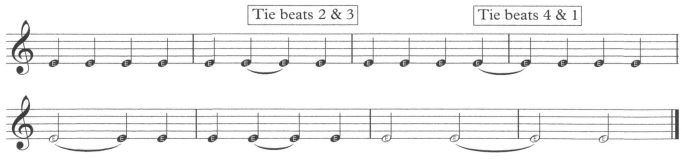

In the exercise above, let's practice playing some tied notes on E.

50

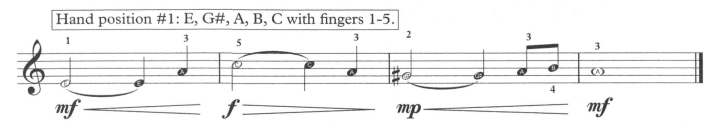

In exercise one on this page, let's play the right-hand melody for the beginning of the piece. Do you see the ties between the first two notes of measures one, two, and three? That means you will hold those sets of half and quarter notes for three beats each.

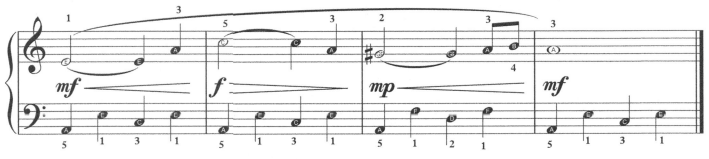

Now, in exercise two, let's put both hands together: the melody in the right hand and the Alberti bass in the left hand. Try playing right hand, then left hand, then both hands for each measure. Then, once you are comfortable, put all four measures together.

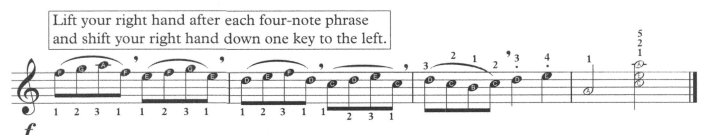

In exercise three, we are going to practice a finger pattern that repeats (going down) on different notes. The commas indicate that you should separate each four-note phrase.

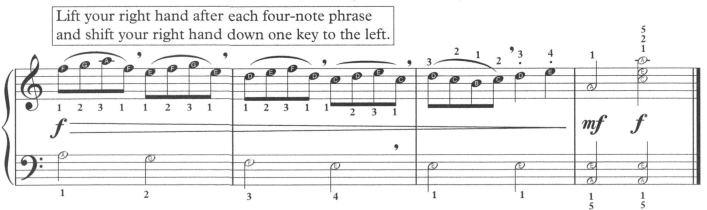

Now, let's put both hands together, in exercise four. As we did before, let's practice right hand, then left hand, then both hands for each measure. After you have the music in your fingers, play all four measures with both hands. As with all of these exercises, start slowly and then gradually build up the speed ("tempo") of the music.

Hungarian Dance

Hand position #1: E, G#, A, B, C with fingers 1-5.

Listen and look for musical patterns in the piece.

Johannes Brahms

Move your thumb to F.

Hand position #2: A, B, C, D, E with fingers 1-5.

Remember that the comma symbol (,) means to lift your hand.

Hand position #3: A, B, C, D, E with fingers 1-5 one octave higher than hand position #2.

Lift your right hand after each four-note phrase and shift your right hand down one key to the left.

Paganini Caprice
Lesson & Overview

Check out video 12

In exercise one, let's practice moving from one chord to the next in the left hand. Start to move to the next chord on beat three of each measure. While your hand is in the air, form the shape of the chord in your hand. This way, you won't have to "scramble" to find the notes of the chord.

For exercise two, let's practice the melody. It starts with the thumb on A and then, in the third measure, goes to a position with the thumb on E.

Let's put both hands together, for exercise three.

In exercise four, we have some sequences to practice. Sequences are musical patterns that repeat on different sets of notes. There are six sequences in this exercise. Can you hear them? (*hint: Each one contains six notes.)

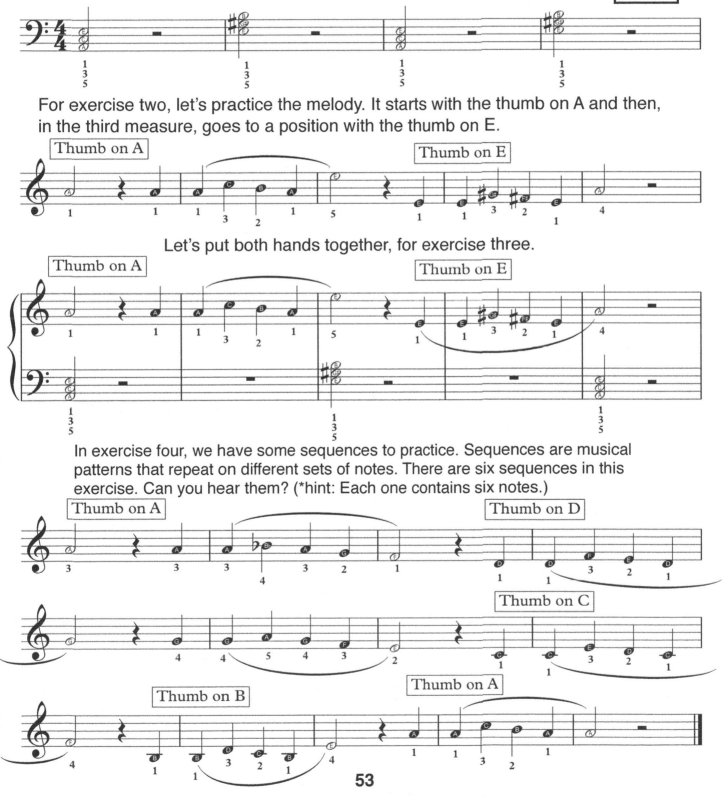

53

Caprice Number 24

Niccolò Paganini

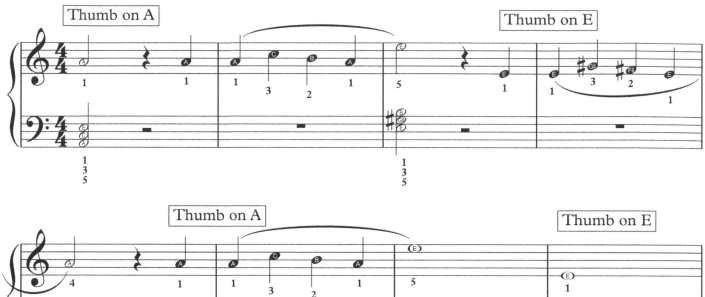

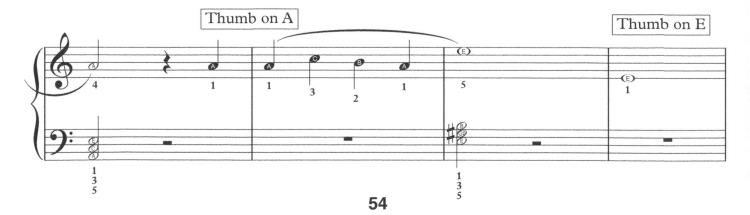

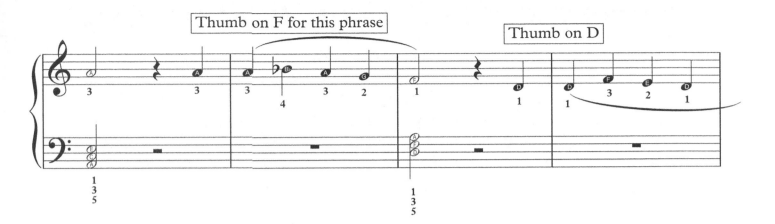

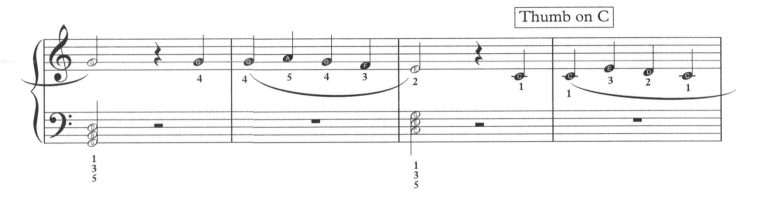

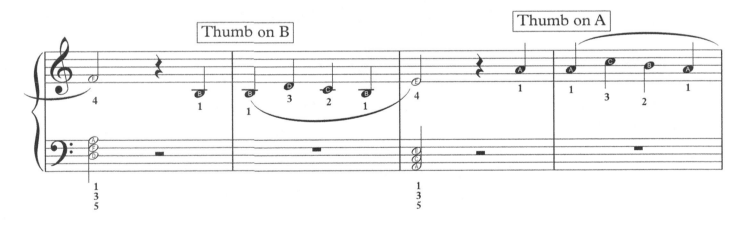

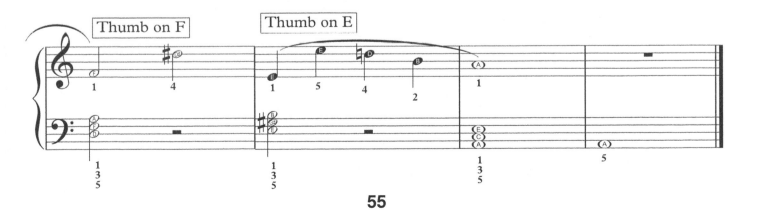

Greensleeves Lesson & Overview

In exercise one, we are going to look at the left-hand technique for *Greensleeves*. Most of the left-hand sections outline chords, played one note at a time. These are called "arpeggios" in music terminology. The word "arpeggio" is Italian and means harp. So, when you are playing this preliminary exercise, try to imagine the piano sounding a little bit like a harp. If possible, let your left-hand wrist drop down a little bit at the beginning of each measure. At the end of each measure, let it raise back to its normal position: parallel to the left hand.

In exercise two, we are gong to focus on the rhythm for the melody in the right hand. We are going to exclude all of the notes of the melody, except for "D". As you take a look at the rhythm for the melody of *Greensleeves,* you will notice that it is in 3/4 time (that is, three quarter notes or their equivalent in each measure) and composed of half notes, quarter notes, eighth notes, and dotted-quarter notes. The dotted quarter notes are equal to one and a half beats. You should count them like this: 1&2. Take a moment to find the note "D" with your right hand thumb and try the exercise. Remember to count the beats and subdivisions (the sections marked between each beat).

Now, in exercise three, let's try playing the right-hand melody of the opening. Please use (and even memorize) the fingering that is listed. As a general guideline, it's best to always strive to use the same fingering once you learn a piece of music. This way, your mind will not have to constantly be figuring out which fingers to place on the keys.

In exercise four, let's take a look at another section of the melody in the right hand. You might notice that the index finger will move over the thumb in measure two. As well, notice the dynamics: forte down to mezzopiano. This means that it will go from loud (relative to the overall sound of the piece) down to fairly soft. When you are playing the piece, starting on the next page, try to make the right hand a little bit louder than the left. This will balance the sound of the piece and bring out the melody.

56

Greensleeves

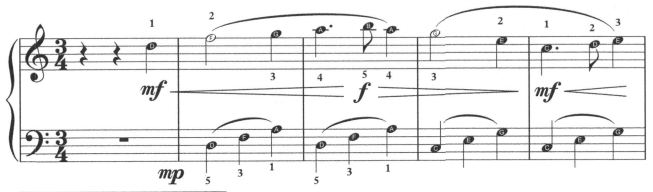

Play the left-hand part softer
than the right-hand part.

Second finger over

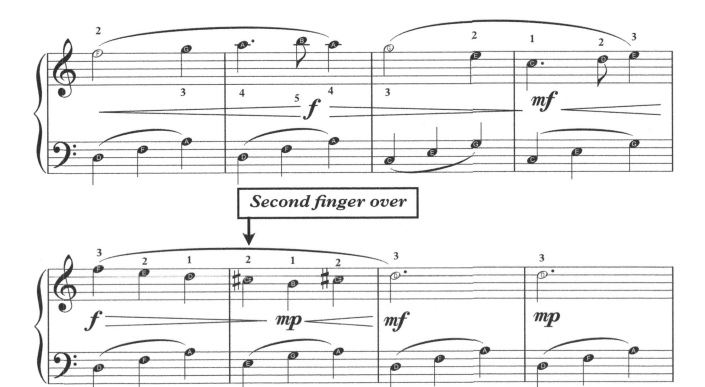

57

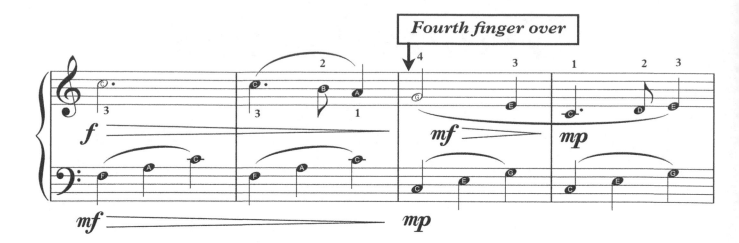

Fourth finger over

Fourth finger over

Second finger over

58

Santa Lucia
(A Classic Neapolitan Song)
Lesson & Overview

In exercise one, let's first take a look at the left hand for this classic Italian song, which was immortalized by an early recording from the great Italian opera singer, Enrico Caruso. The song is in 3/4 time; so, make sure you have a steady three count (1, 2, 3) going in your mind or aloud for each measure. As you are practicing this left-hand exercise, try to create the dynamic flow, going from mezzo-forte (medium loud) to forte (loud), and then down to mezzo-piano (medium soft). The dots above or below the notes are staccato symbols. Staccato means bouncy or detached. Try to give this left hand part a bouncy feel.

Exercise #1

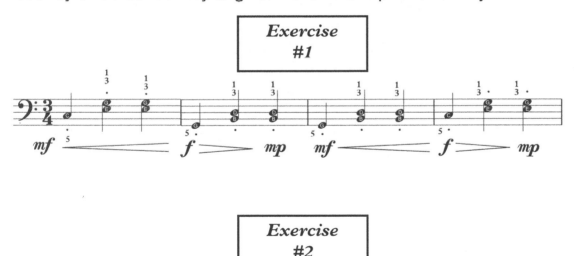

Exercise #2

Now, in exercise two, let's practice the right-hand melody. At the start of each slur (the curved line that goes over the notes in measures one and three) drop your right wrist; lift up your right wrist (parallel to your hand) on the second note of the phrase.

59

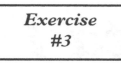

Exercise
#3

For exercise three, let's put both hands together. Remember to practice slowly and count the beats aloud or in your mind. Try to make the left hand a little bouncy and the right hand a little bit smooth.

Exercise
#4

Exercise four will use a similar wrist technique as exercise two. At the beginning of the slur, drop your right wrist down a little bit. Then, lift the wrist back to the position parallel to the right hand on the second note of the slur (or phrase). There are four slurs in the first two measures: E and C, C and G, G and E, and F and D.

Exercise
#5

In exercise five, let's put both hands together. Focus mainly on the right-hand part. The last note of the piece is a low C (two octaves below middle C). You should play it with the fifth finger of your left hand.

Santa Lucia

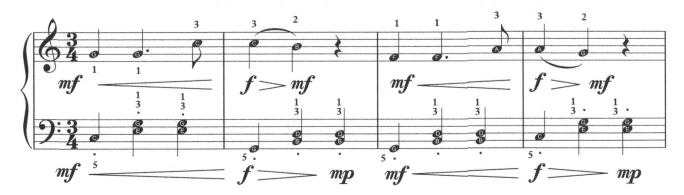

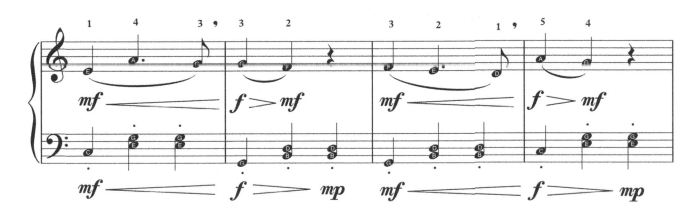

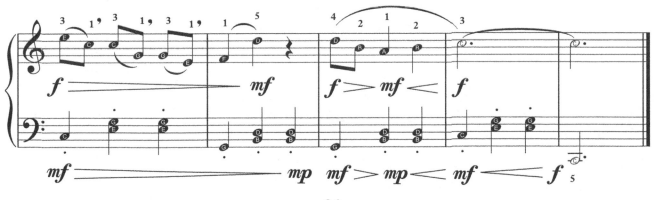

Lesson & Overview on Grieg's Hall of the Mountain King

Hall of the Mountain King is a fun and energetic piece to play. If you are not familiar with the music, please download and listen to the MP3 audio file from the SteeplechaseMusic website.

In exercise one, we are going to practice the Alberti bass figures for the left hand. Please notice that the position changes in the fourth measure. There is a new symbol in this piece: **8vb**. This symbol and the bracket that follows it indicates that we should play one octave (eight notes) lower than what is written. There is a corresponding symbol: **8va**. When you see this symbol, play an octave (eight notes) higher than written.

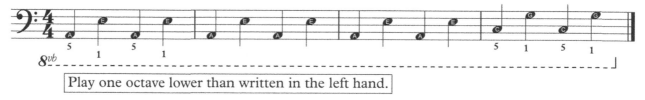

Play one octave lower than written in the left hand.

We will now move to the right hand, for exercise two. Please note that the piece starts in the bass clef for the right hand and gradually rises up into the treble clef for the right hand. For the first two and a half measures, we will stay in a position around the notes A, B, C, D and E. Halfway through measure three, we will change to a new position. This right hand pattern will repeat throughout the piece.

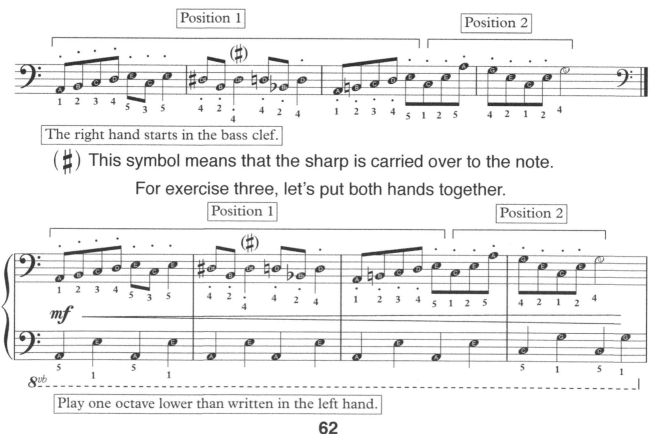

The right hand starts in the bass clef.

(♯) This symbol means that the sharp is carried over to the note.

For exercise three, let's put both hands together.

Play one octave lower than written in the left hand.

62

In exercise four, let's practice this melody for the right hand. The first five notes of the melody fit comfortably under the hand; you will play part of an ascending (going up) A Minor scale (the notes A, B, C, D and E). On the sixth note of the melody, your hand will change positions and your fingers will need to spread out a little bit more. Also notice that the dynamics go from mezzo-forte (medium loud) to forte (loud). Try to play this melody in a smooth, legato manner, as opposed to the staccato (bouncy) style for the right hand in the previous exercise.

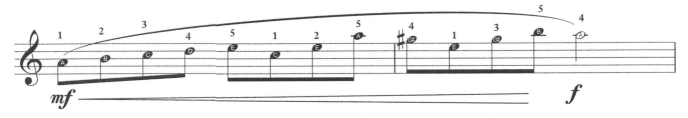

The first two measures of exercise five have dissonant ("spicy" or "agitated") chords. We also have accents (>) over the chords. Accents give a sudden jolt of energy to the music. In the left hand, you will play the notes C, Eb and Gb for the chord. Try playing each measure of this exercise hands alone. Then put both hands together for each measure. Finally, play the whole exercise with both hands.

Give an accent on the second beat.

Play these two measures legato (smooth).

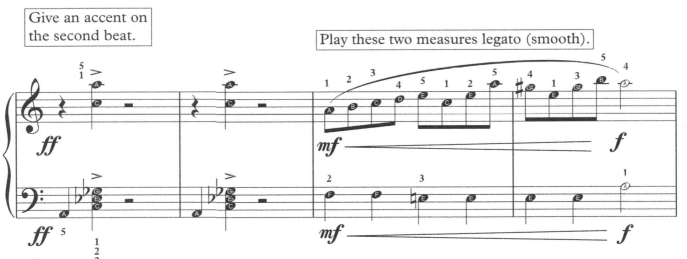

Exercise six starts with a long, A Minor scale that goes from the left hand up to the right hand. On the sixth note of the scale, the third finger of your left hand will need to go over your thumb. In the second measure, the scale will continue in the right hand. Practice this exercise slowly to build up your coordination.

These two measures are one big A Minor scale.

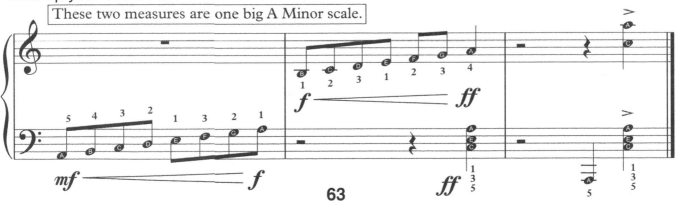

Hall of the Mountain King

Edvard Grieg

The right hand starts in the bass clef.

Listen for the repeated patterns throughout the piece.

Play one octave lower than written in the left hand.

Play one octave higher than written in the right hand.

Play one octave lower than written in the left hand.

Change to treble clef.

Play one octave lower than written in the left hand.

Play one octave lower than written in the left hand.

64

Give an accent on the second beat.

Play these two measures legato (smooth).

Play these two measures legato (smooth).

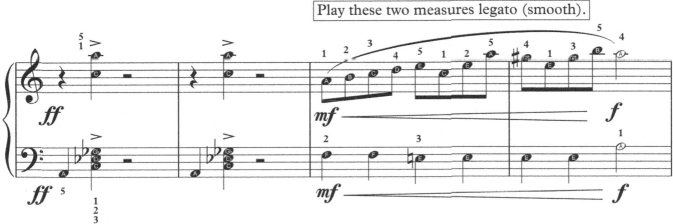

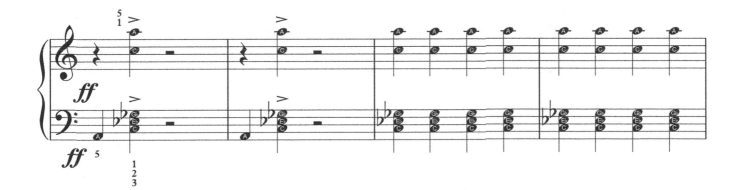

These two measures are one big A Minor scale.

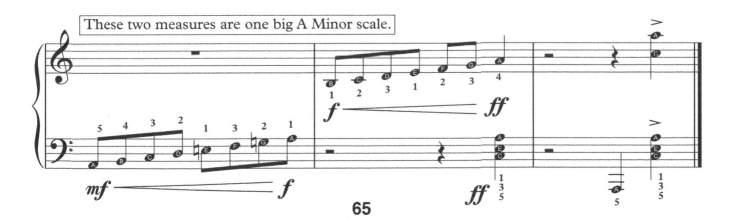

65

Purcell Minuet: Overview & Lesson

A minuet is a stately dance form in 3/4 time. When you play a minuet, take a moderate tempo: not too fast and not too slow. In exercise one, let's practice the first four measures of Purcell's minuet in the right hand.

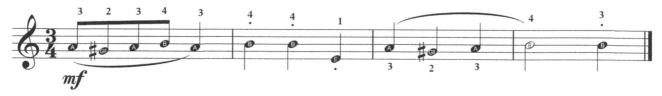

Now, in exercise two, let's practice the first four measures of the left hand.

For exercise three, let's put both hands together. Practice this slowly, at first. It is all right if you would like to practice and each measure by repeating the measure several times.

In exercise four, let's work on the right-hand part for the second system of music. You might notice that there are some similar patterns between exercises one and four.

For exercise five, let's put both hands together.

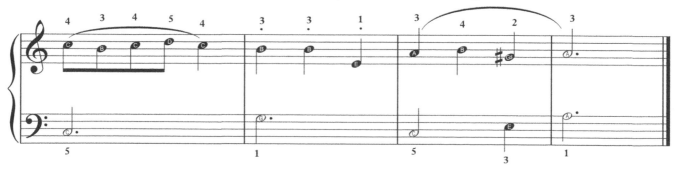

66

Minuet

Henry Purcell

Andante

J.S. Bach Prelude in C Major: Overview & Arpeggios

In this lesson, we are going to prepare for playing the *C Major Prelude* by J.S. Bach. Arpeggios are one of the key concepts at work in this piece. The term "arpeggio" comes from the Italian word "arpa", which means "harp". Along these lines, an arpeggio is a chord played one note at a time, instead of a chord where all of the notes are played at once. This style of playing one note at a time mimics the sound of a harp.

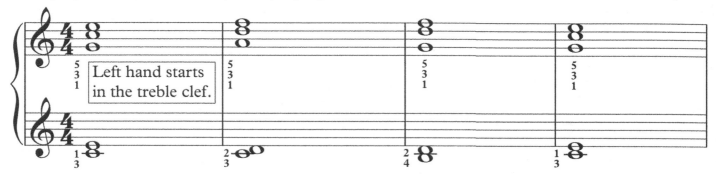

Let's start by playing the first eight measures as chords, rather than arpeggios. Once you are comfortable with the fingering, try playing the first four measures as arpeggios (one note at a time). This method of reducing the arpeggios to block chords can be done for the entire piece and will make it easier to learn.

Prelude in C Major

Check out video 13

Adagio — Try to bring out the top note of each measure.

J.S. Bach

Left hand starts in the treble clef.

This measure has the same fingering as the previous one. This two-measure pattern occurs for the whole piece.

These two measures are the same as the first two in the piece. They act as a kind of "little ending", before the music moves in a different harmonic direction.

These are high A notes.

The F# repeats in this measure.

The F# repeats in this measure too.

69

This is the B
below middle C.

The F# repeats
in this measure.

This is the A
below middle C.

This is the A
below middle C.

The left hand will go into
the bass clef in this measure.

Slow down a little bit in the last two measures.
This will indicate that the piece is ending.

Swan Lake Theme

Pyotr Ilyich
Tchaikovsky

Andante

For each measure, count: 1 & 2 & 3 & 4 &. This is the rhythm of the left hand for the entire piece.

This type of left-hand pattern is used throughout the piece.

You will use fingers five and one for most of the piece in the left hand. If there are no finger numbers marked for the left hand, you should use finger numbers five and one (pinky and thumb).

The melody goes from the right hand to the left hand and back in this measure.

The melody goes from the right hand to the left hand and back in this measure.

The thumb goes under on the A.

This is a reminder to play Bb.

The third finger goes over here.

The thumb goes under on the A.

This is a reminder to play Bb.

The left hand goes down to a low E. Use fingers five and one.

The melody goes below middle C in this measure.

Gymnopedie

Erik Satie

For this gentle piece, remember to count to three for each measure. Try the left hand alone, first. Then, try the right hand alone. Slowly, play with both hands together; it might be best to play hands together for groups of four measures, following the melody.

Adagio

Make the left-hand part a little quieter than the right-hand part.

73

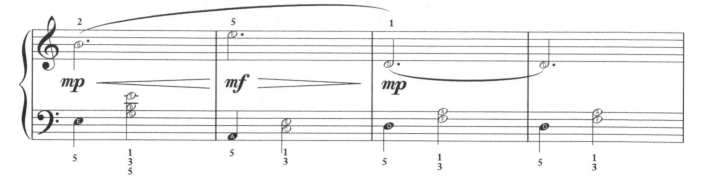

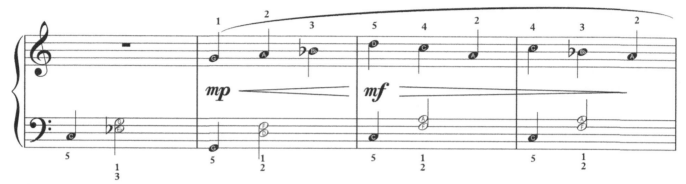

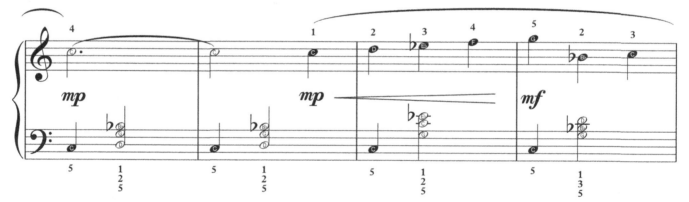

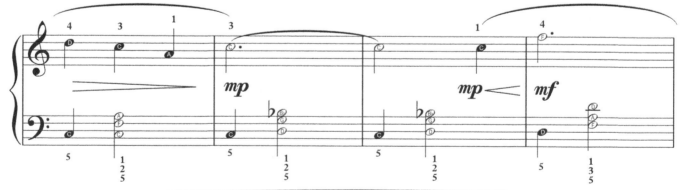

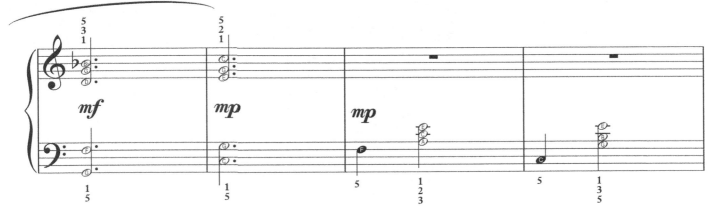

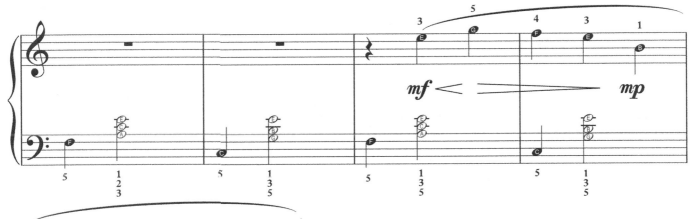

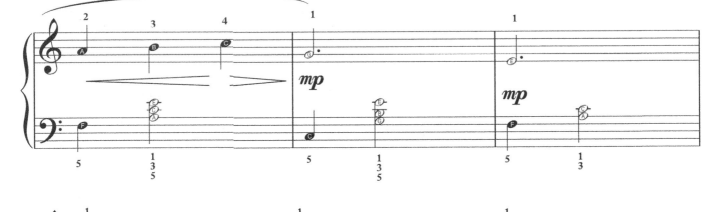

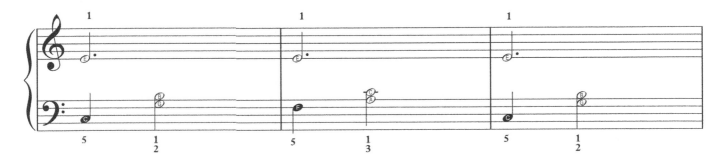

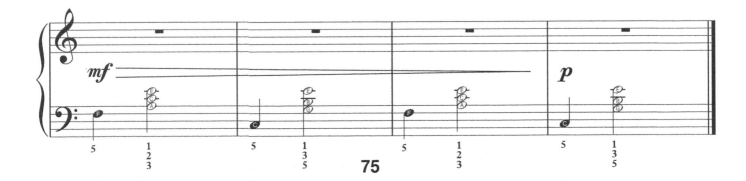

Canon

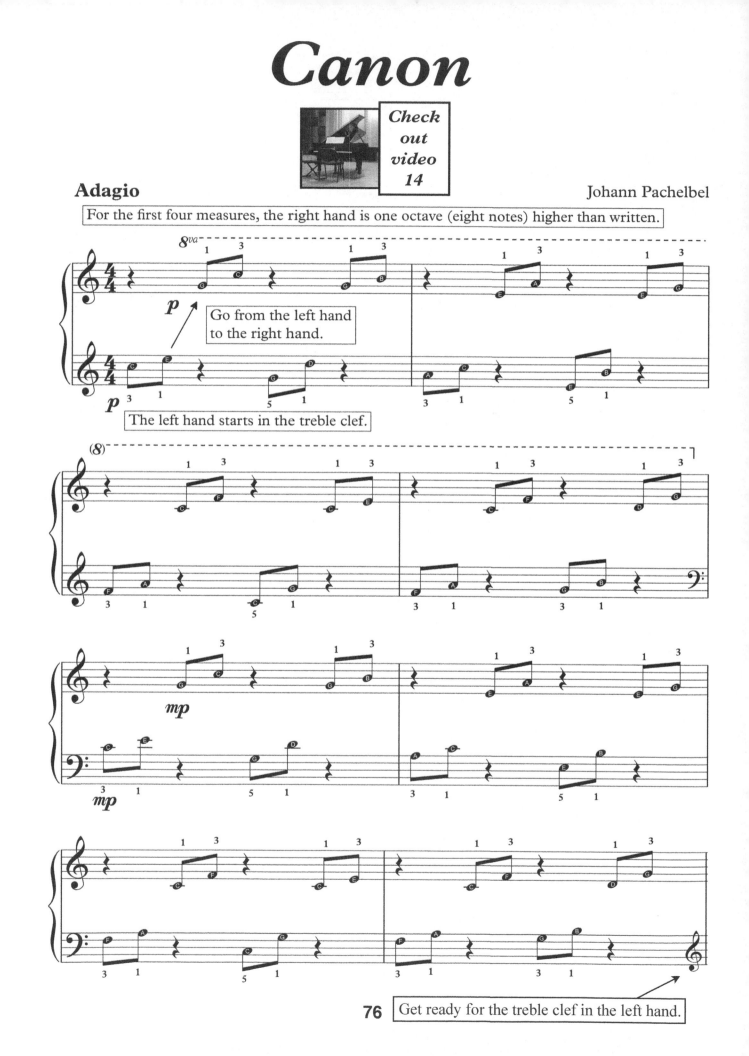

Check out video 14

Adagio

Johann Pachelbel

For the first four measures, the right hand is one octave (eight notes) higher than written.

Go from the left hand to the right hand.

The left hand starts in the treble clef.

Get ready for the treble clef in the left hand.

76

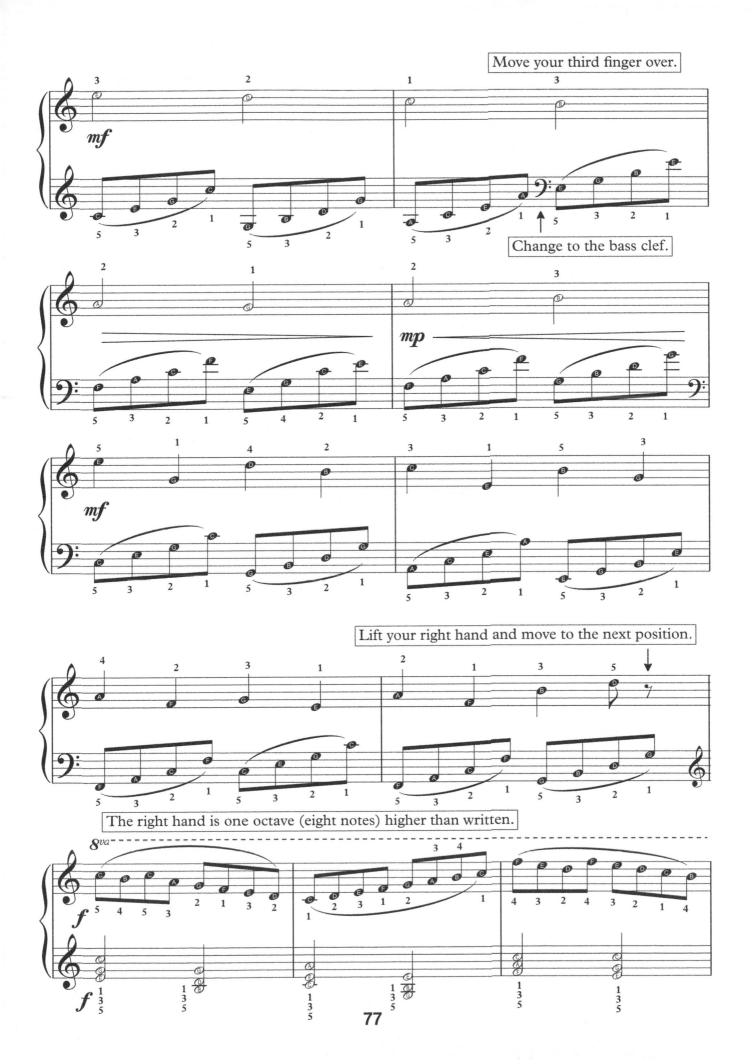

Move your third finger over.

Change to the bass clef.

Lift your right hand and move to the next position.

The right hand is one octave (eight notes) higher than written.

77

Lift your right hand.

Lift your right hand.

Go from the right hand to the left hand.

The left hand is in the treble clef

Second finger over

The left hand is in the bass clef

78

The Wedding March

Felix Mendelssohn

Allegro

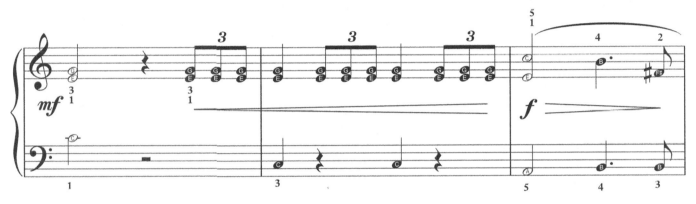

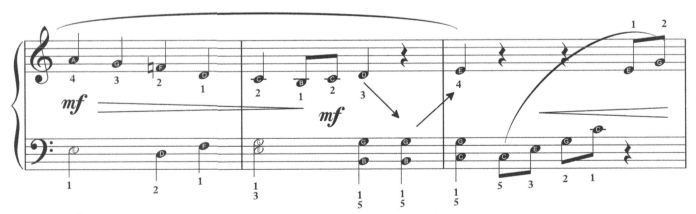

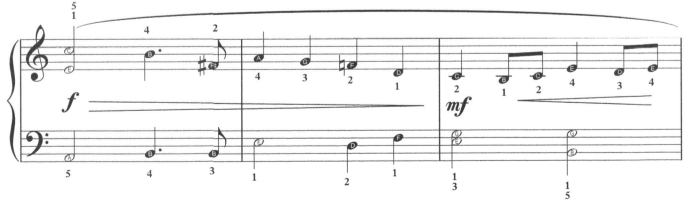

79

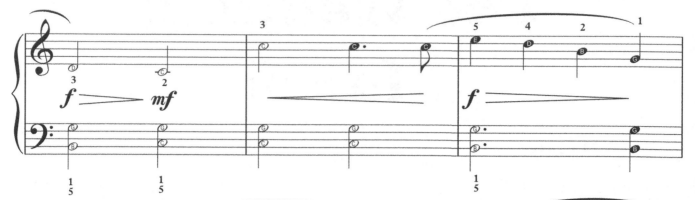

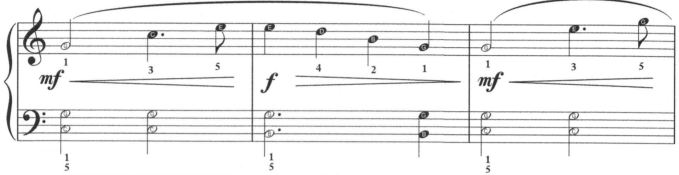

Minuet in G Minor

For this piece by Bach, practice one hand at a time in groups of four measures. Take one system (line) of music at a time. Then, play with both hands in four-measure groups. Remember to count to three for each measure.

Andante

J.S. Bach

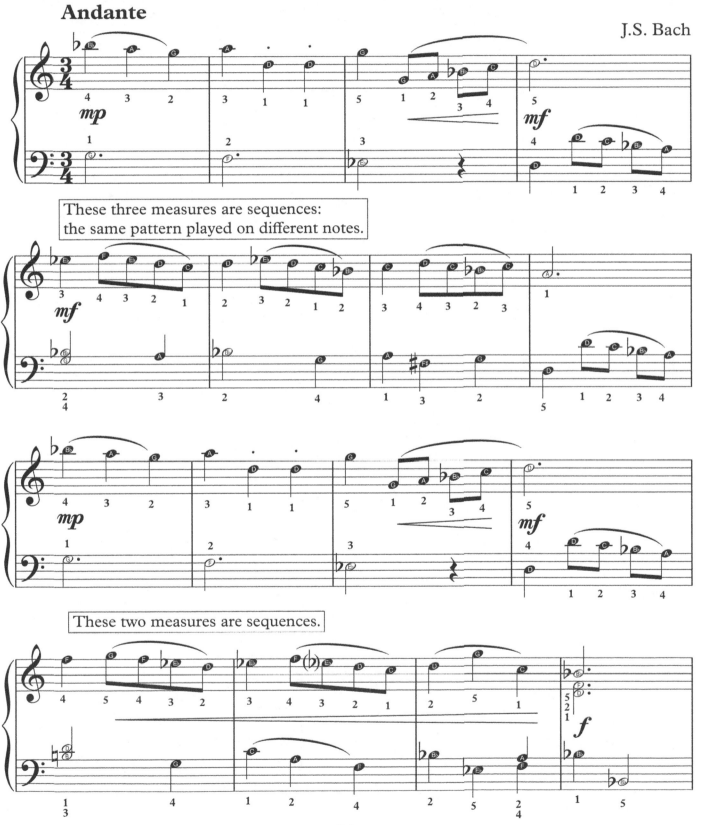

These three measures are sequences: the same pattern played on different notes.

These two measures are sequences.

81

Bring out the contrasting sounds between legato (smooth) notes and staccato (detached) notes.

Drop the right-hand wrist for the first note of each two-note group in this bar.

82

Dance of the Mirlitons
(from *The Nutcracker*)

The dots indicate staccato
(or "bouncy") notes

Suddenly loud

Third finger over

Pyotr Ilyich
Tchaikovsky

Suddenly loud

83

Tales of Hoffmann

This famous piece by Offenbach is in 6/8 time. Each eighth note counts as a beat. You may count 1, 2, 3, 4, 5, 6 for each measure. Please note that the left-hand part often outlines a chord in an "um-pah-pah" style or arpeggiates it.

Jacques Offenbach

"um pah pah" "um pah pah"

arpeggiated chords

Lift your hand here.

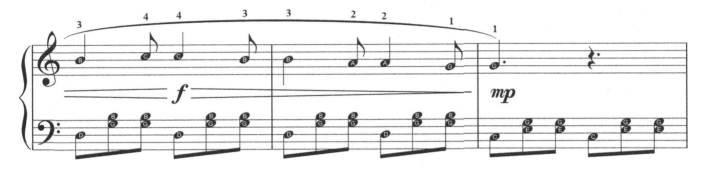

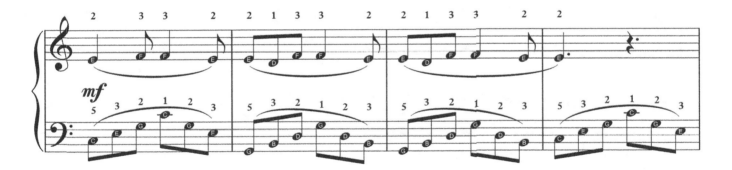

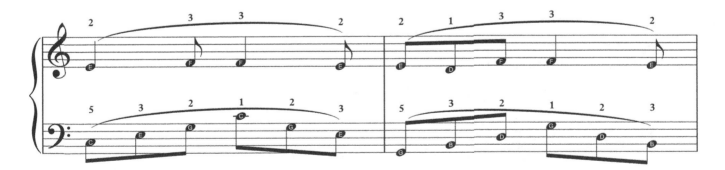

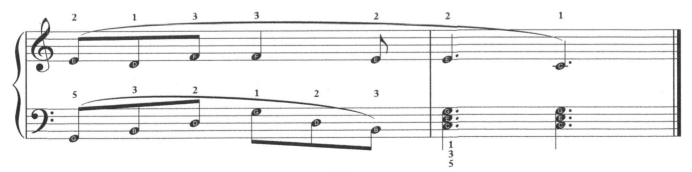

Eine kleine Nachtmusik

To help us play this wonderful piece by Mozart, we are going to focus on subdividing (counting the halfway points between each beat). Since the piece is in 4/4 time, we count, "1 & 2 & 3 & 4 &", for each measure. Practice one measure at a time: right hand, left hand, then both hands. Gradually put two measures together; then, put four measures together and continue in this manner.

Wolfgang Amadeus Mozart

Allegro

Throughout the piece, drop your right-hand wrist for the first note of each two-note slur.

Make the left hand softer than the right hand.

86

Subdivide here.
Count: 1 & 2 & 3 & 4 &.

Subdivide here too.
Count: 1 & 2 & 3 & 4 &.

The right hand goes into the bass clef here.

Hungarian Dance

In studying this famous piece by Franz Liszt, first learn the left-hand part for the first page. The regularity of the rhythm will help you keep an even beat. For the first two systems in the right hand, you will have a repeated rhythmic figure. Try counting, "1, 2, 3, 4, &", for each of these first seven measures. When you first start working on the scale figures on page two, play one hand at a time. Have fun!

Franz Liszt

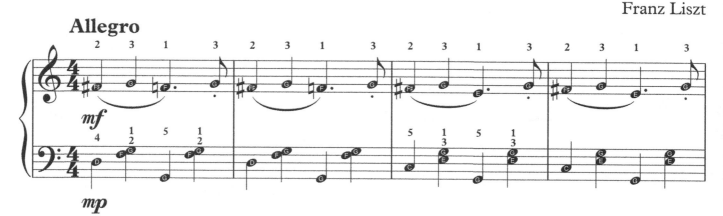

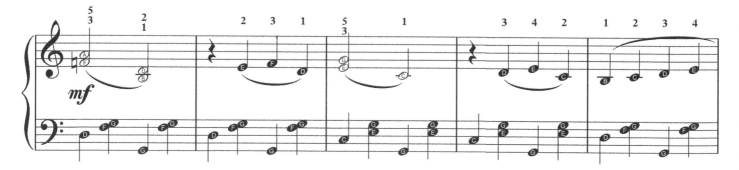

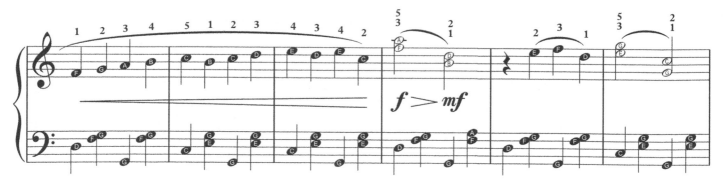

88

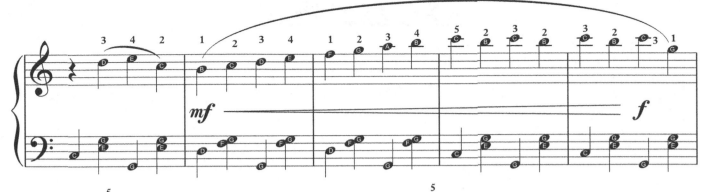

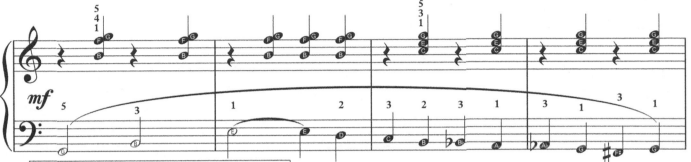

Bring out the melody in the left hand.

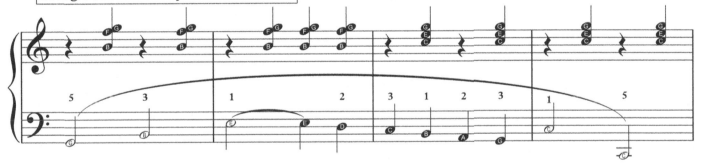

Drop your wrists on the first note of each two-note phrase.

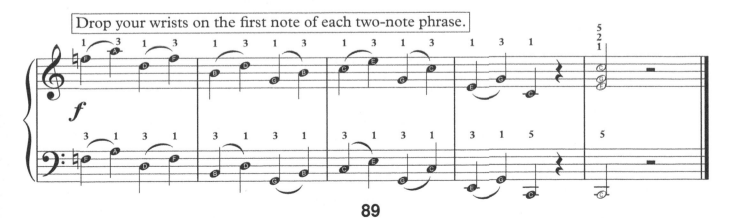

Bourrée

J.S. Bach

The right hand goes into the bass clef.

The right hand goes into the bass clef.

The right hand goes into the bass clef.

The right hand goes into the bass clef.

90

Hark the Herald Angels Sing

Felix Mendelssohn

Andante

91

Air

This lyrical piece by Purcell is marked quarter note equals eighty-four. This means that the tempo ("speed") of the piece is at eighty-four beats per minute. If you don't have a metronome, you can find many free or very inexpensive digital metronomes and metronome apps online.

There are four systems ("lines") in this piece. In your practicing, it might be best if you play the first measure of a system (right hand, left hand, then both hands). Once you have the first measure down, follow the same process with the second, third, and fourth measures in the system. Once you have mastered each individual measure, play two-measure groups. For example, play measures one and two. Then, play measures three and four. Then play all four measures.

Henry Purcell

The Blue Danube Waltz

This famous piece is a waltz; so, it is in 3/4 time. Make sure that you count, "1, 2, 3", for each measure. Your left hand will do the job of keeping the time in an "um-pah-pah" style. There are three main types of chords for the left hand: C Major (the notes C, E, G), G Dominant Seventh (the notes G, B, D, F), and F Major (the notes F, A, C). Some of the chord forms for the left hand leave out a note or two, especially the G Dominant Seventh forms.

The right hand alternates between staccato (bouncy) and legato (smooth) notes and phrases. Try to bring out the contrast between the bouncy and smooth notes. The legato phrases often outline chords and their inversions played one note at a time, for example C Major (C, E, G) or G Major in first inversion (B, D, G).

At first, learn one system of music at a time, rather than practicing the entire piece. Listen to the interplay between the right and left hand part. One of the great things about playing the piano is that we can have fun exploring the interaction between the musical figures played in each hand. It's a little like being our own mini orchestra.

Johann Strauss

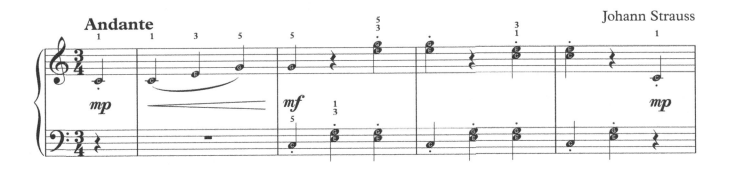

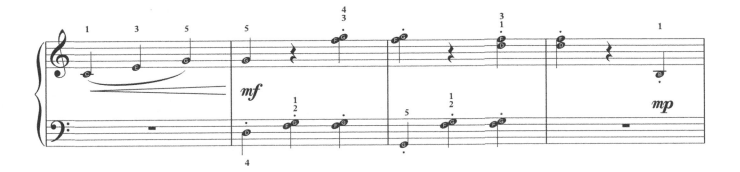

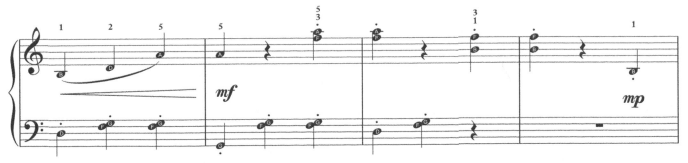

93

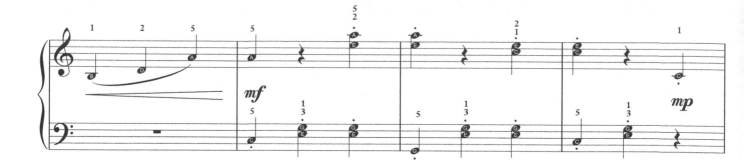

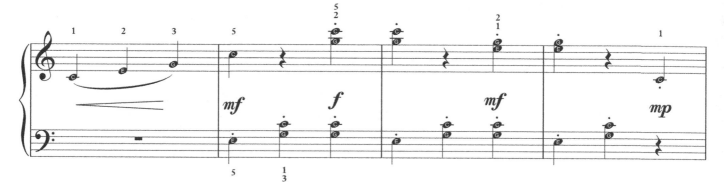

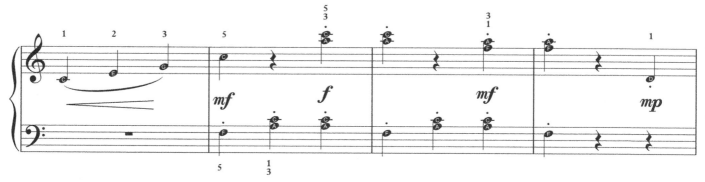

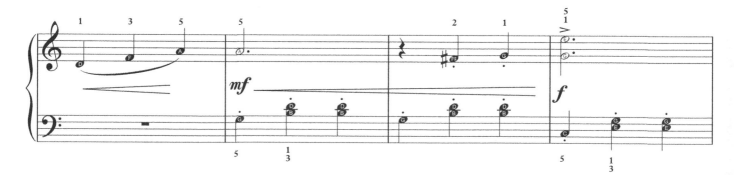

Third Piano Concerto Theme

This dramatic concerto theme from Beethoven starts out loud and gets louder. Have fun bringing out the energy of the opening theme, which is doubled in octaves in both hands. Then, in measures three and four, decrease the dynamics and bring out the character of the staccato notes and the accents.

In systems two, three, and four, you might notice small numbers above the treble clef. These are measure numbers. In measures five through eight, learn right-hand and left-hand parts separately, first. Then, once you are comfortable with the music, play both hands together for these measures. In measures nine through fourteen, you might notice a descending scale pattern in the three phrases for the right hand. For the last three measures of the piece, practice each hand separately, before putting them both together.

Ludwig van Beethoven

Minuet in G

Check out video 15

J.S. Bach

Andante

Thumb Under

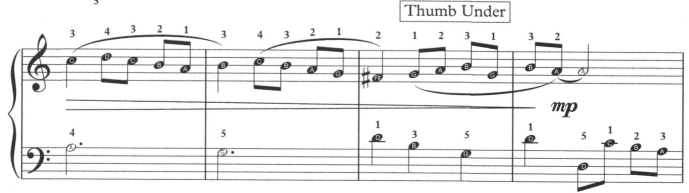

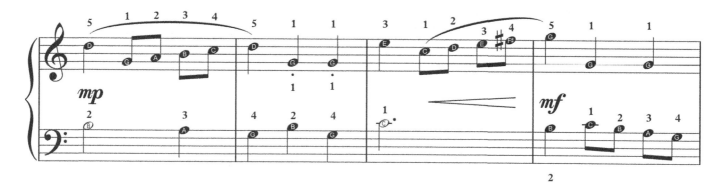

Second Finger Over

96

Bring out the contrasting sounds between legato (smooth) notes and staccato (detached) notes.

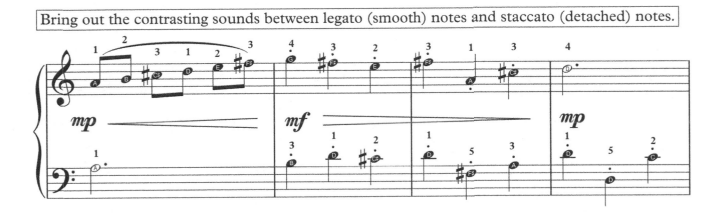

Drop the right-hand wrist
for the first note of each
three-note group in these bars.

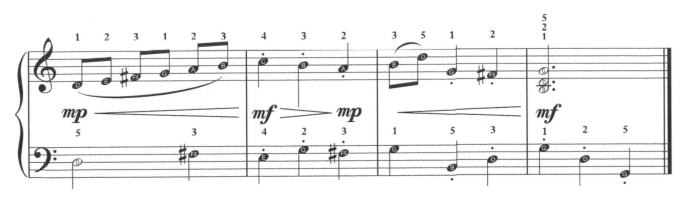

97

Hallelujah

George Frideric Handel

$\quad \downarrow = 100$

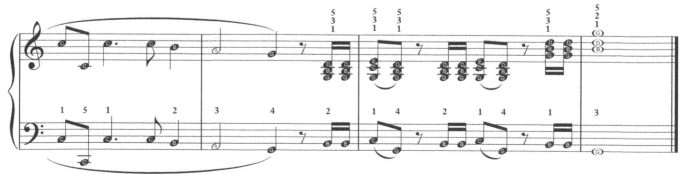

Turkish Rondo

♩ = 100

Wolfgang Amadeus Mozart

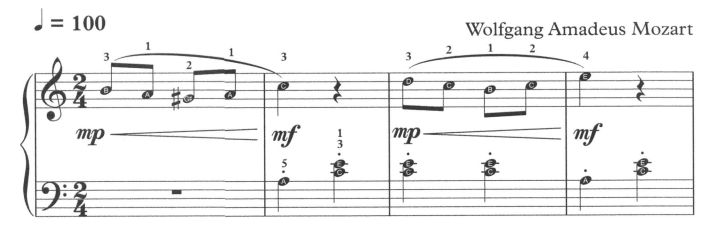

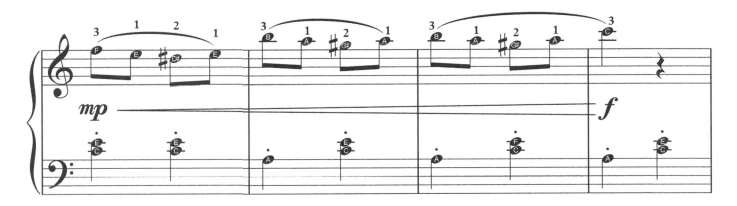

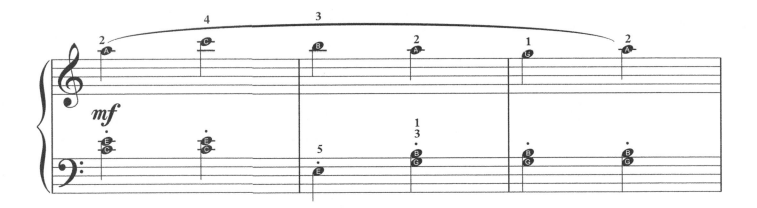

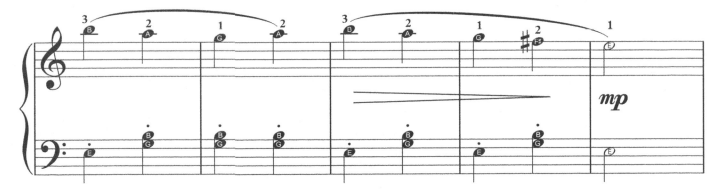

99

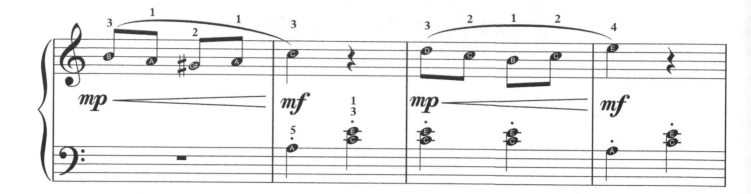

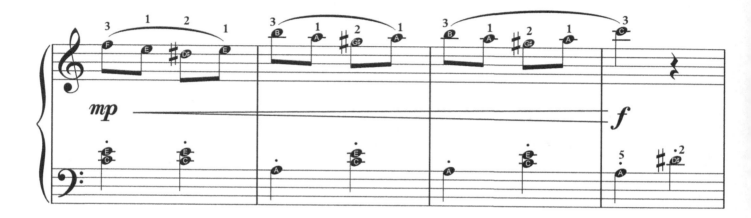

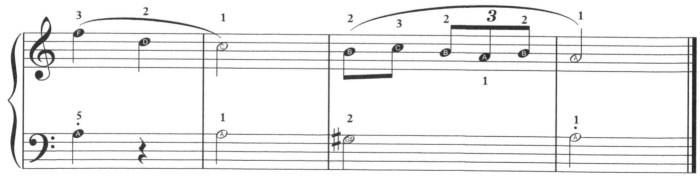

Overview on Sixteenth Notes

A sixteenth note is one fourth of a quarter note. In other words, you need four sixteenth notes to equal one quarter note. Sixteenth notes have two beams (or flags); this distinguishes them from other notes, like eighth notes, which have one beam (or flag). In the following exercises, we are going to practice the most common combinations for sixteenth notes. For these exercises, we are only playing the notes on middle C.

In the first exercise, let's play and count four quarter notes and then play and count groups of four sixteenth notes. When we count groups of four sixteenth notes, we say, "1 e & a". The first number of each group indicates the beat. For example the "2" in "2 e & a" indicates the second beat of the measure. The "3" in "3 e & a" indicates the third beat of the measure.

In the second exercise, let's play and count four quarter notes and then play and count groups of four eighth notes and sixteenth notes.

In the third exercise, let's play and count four quarter notes and then play and count another combination of groups of four eighth notes and sixteenth notes.

In the fourth exercise, let's play and count four quarter notes and then play and count groups of four dotted-eighth notes and sixteenth notes.

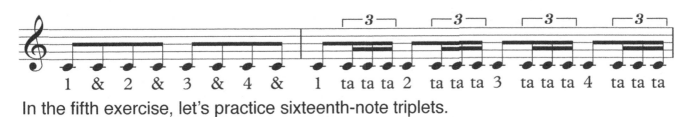

In the fifth exercise, let's practice sixteenth-note triplets.

101

The Toreador Song

Georges Bizet

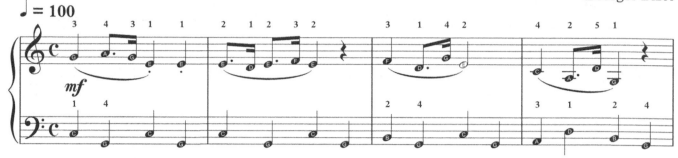

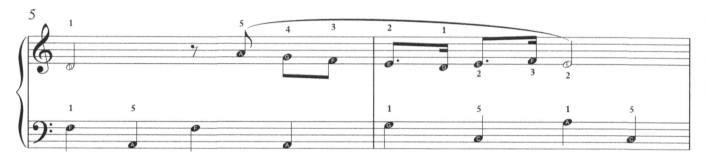

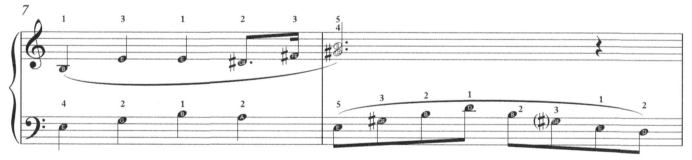

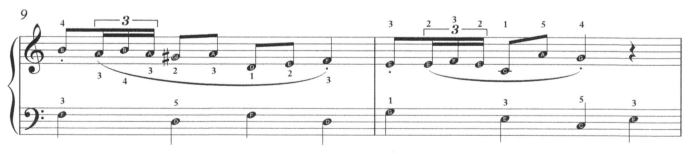

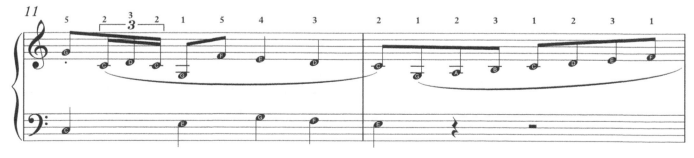

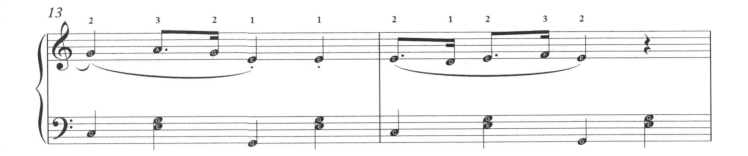

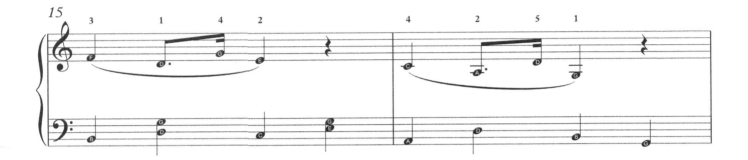

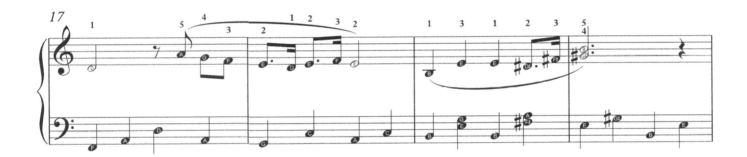

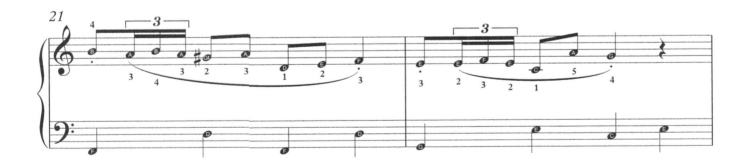

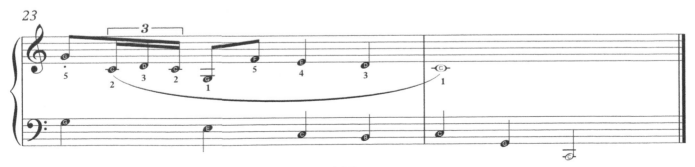

La donna è mobile

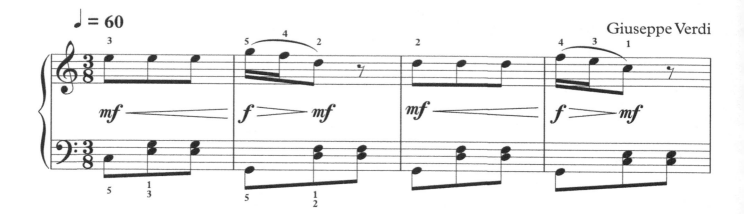

Giuseppe Verdi

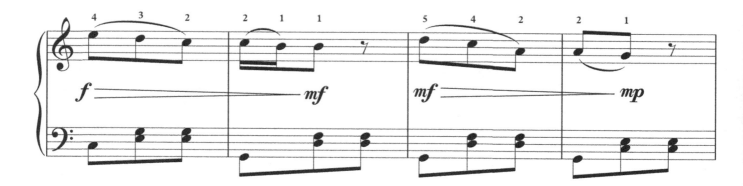

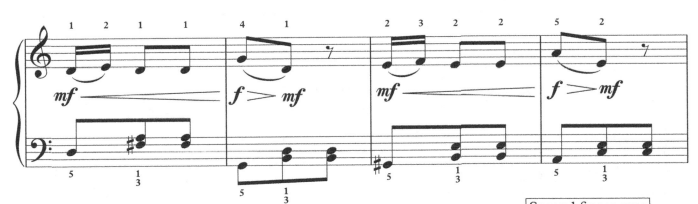

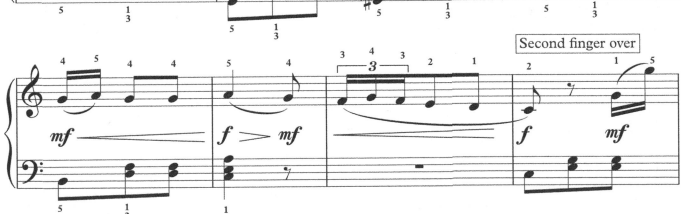

Second finger over

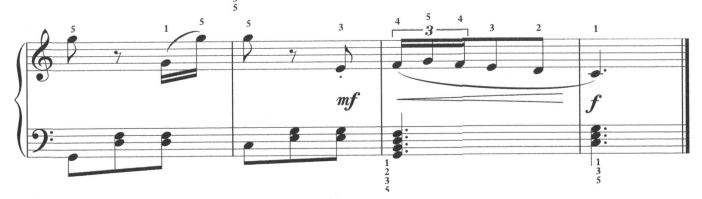

5th Symphony Theme

$\quad \quad = 100$

Ludwig van Beethoven

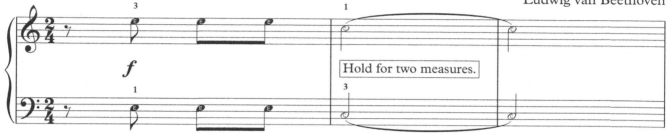

Hold for two measures.

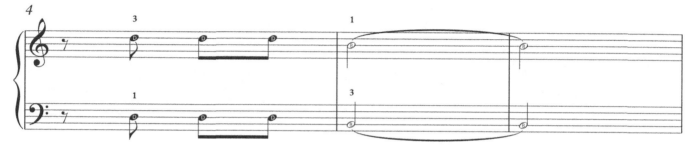

The arrow indicates to go from right to left hand with the melody.

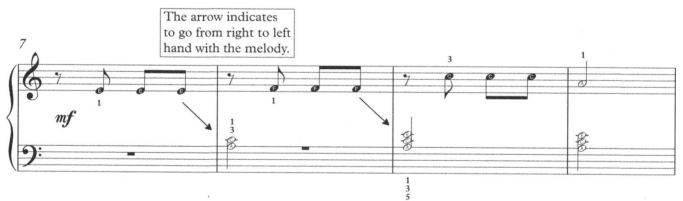

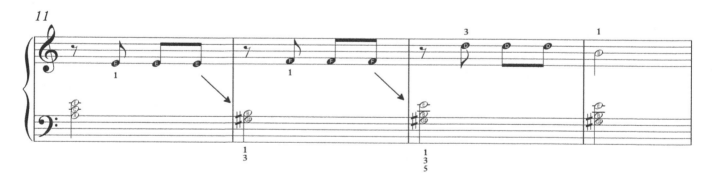

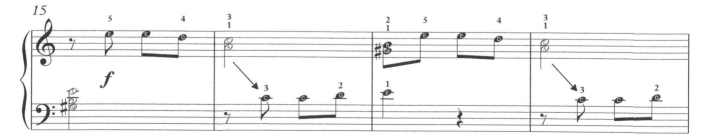

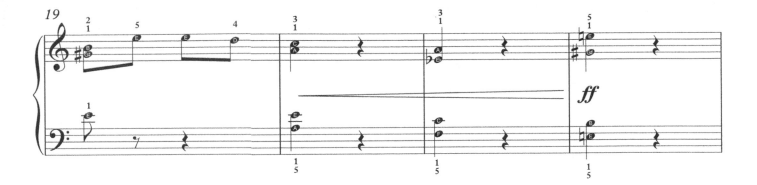

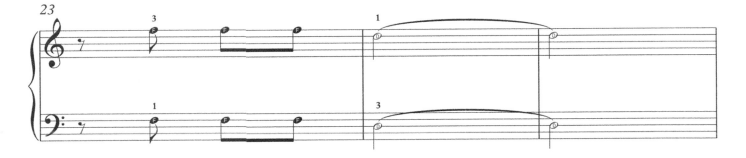

The hands will "leap frog" over one another here.

Change to treble clef. Change to bass clef.

The hands will again "leap frog" over one another here.

Change to treble clef. Change to bass clef.

107

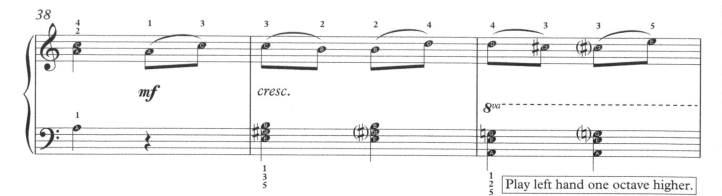

Play left hand one octave higher.

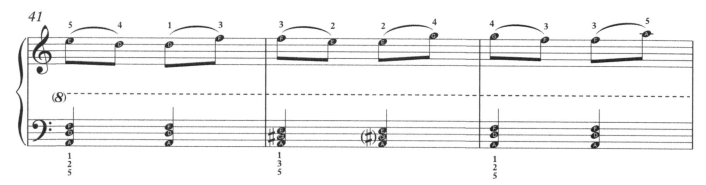

Change to treble clef.

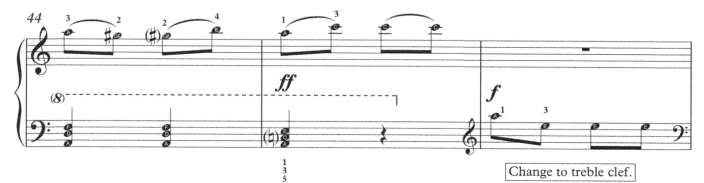

Change to bass clef.

Prelude

Frédéric Chopin

Place your thumb over the notes A and B.

Place your thumb over the notes A and B.

The Wild Horseman

Check out video 16

Robert Schumann

$\quad = 100$

Remember the accents.

110

Orfeo ed Euridice

Christoph Willibald Gluck

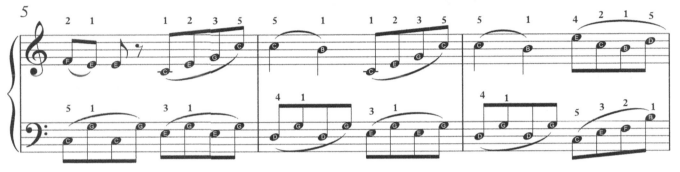

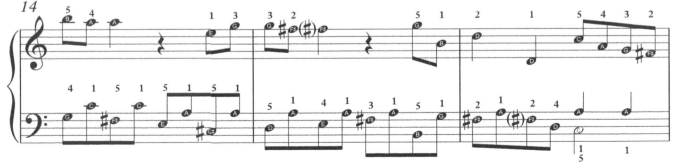

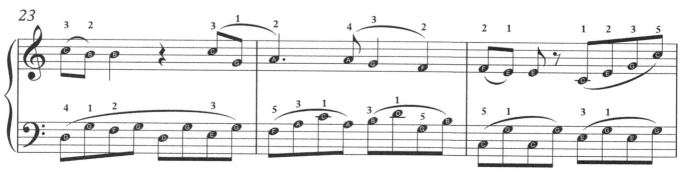

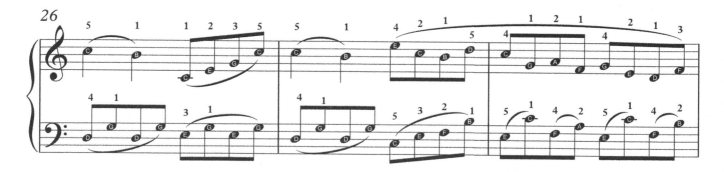

Intermezzo from Cavalleria Rusticana

In the first eight measures of this beautifully lyrical piece, you may be a little bit flexible about the rhythm. You may "stretch" the time to follow the flow of the melody in this eight-measure introduction. In music, we use the term "rubato" (which means "stolen" in Italian) to indicate a free, rhythmic feel. It's as if we "steal" a little time. Try it out and have fun!

Pietro Mascagni

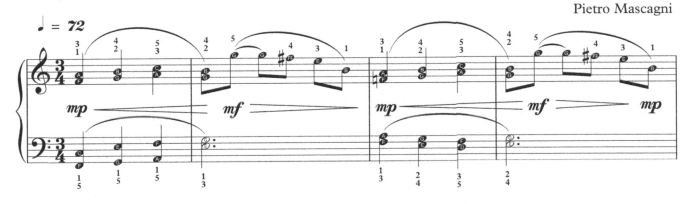

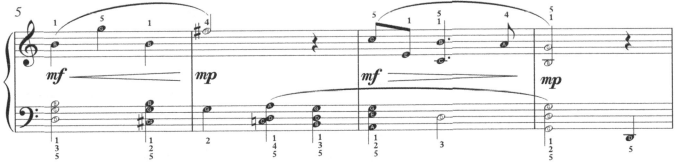

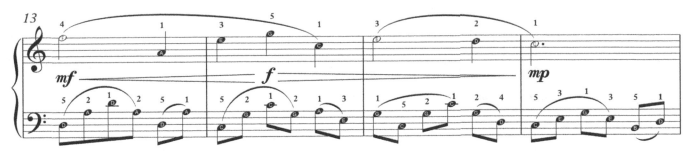

113

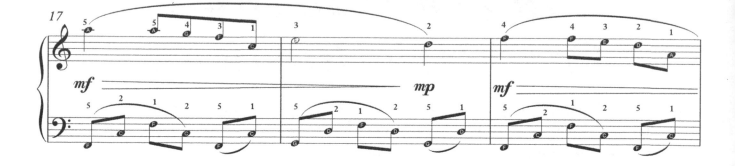

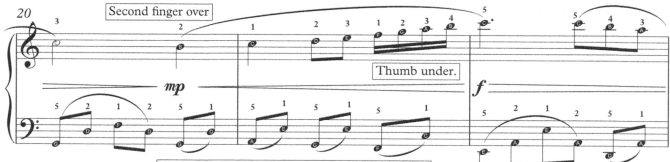

Second finger over

Thumb under.

Bring out this descending bassline: G, A, G, F, E.
This will create a beautiful and dramatic effect!

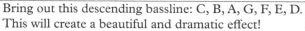

Bring out this descending bassline: C, B, A, G, F, E, D.
This will create a beautiful and dramatic effect!

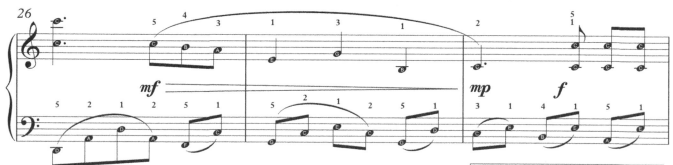

Bring out this descending bassline
in the measures 28 & 29:
C, B, A, G, F, E, F.

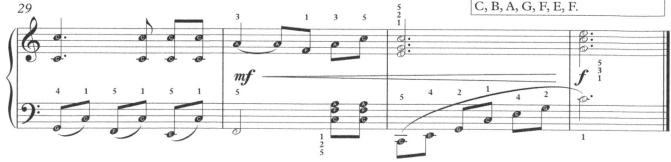

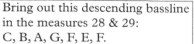

Für Elise

Ludwig van Beethoven

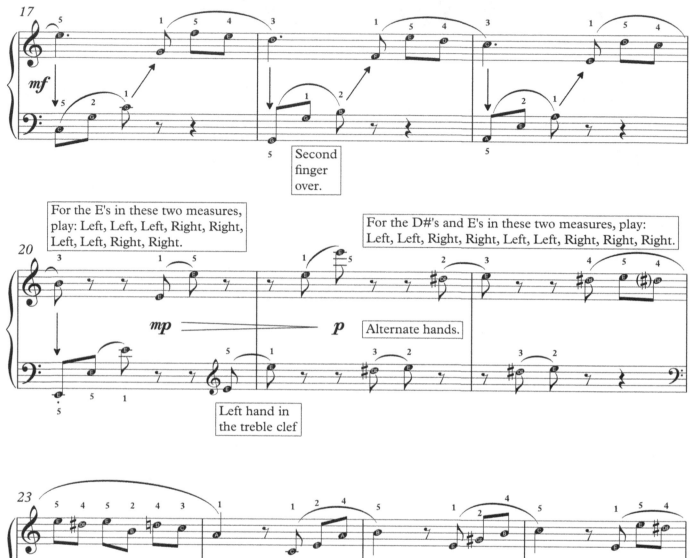

Second finger over.

For the E's in these two measures, play: Left, Left, Left, Right, Right, Left, Left, Right, Right.

For the D#'s and E's in these two measures, play: Left, Left, Right, Right, Left, Left, Right, Right, Right.

Alternate hands.

Left hand in the treble clef

Second finger over.

Sonatina in C: First Movement

Muzio Clementi

Check out video 18

$\quad = 120$

Bring out the staccato notes.

Drop, then lift your wrist.

Drop, then lift your wrist.

This is a repeat symbol. Go back to measure one.

117

Bring out the left-hand melody.

Drop, then lift your wrist.

Drop, then lift your wrist.

This is a repeat symbol. Go back to measure 16.

Sonatina in C: Second Movement

Check out video 19

For the triplets, remember to count "123, 223, 323" for each measure.

Bring out the melody in the right hand.

Drop your wrist at the beginning of each triplet.

See the video lesson for the trill style.

Go from the left hand to the right hand here.

119

Bring out the melody in the right hand.

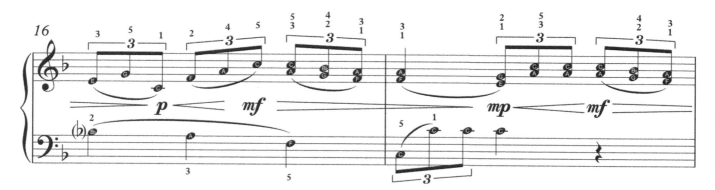

Bring out the melody in the right hand.

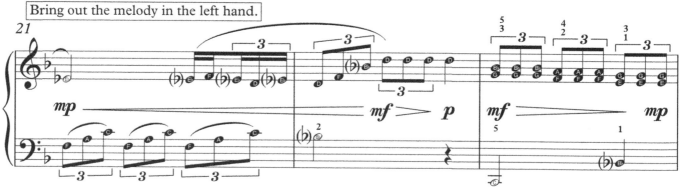

Bring out the melody in the left hand.

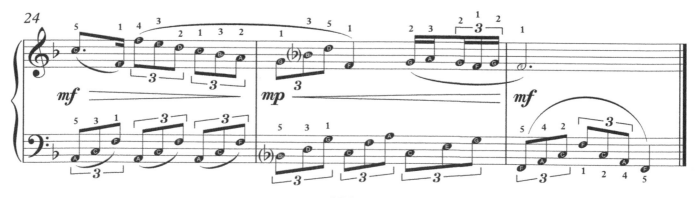

Check out video 20

Sonatina in C: Third Movement

♩ = 100

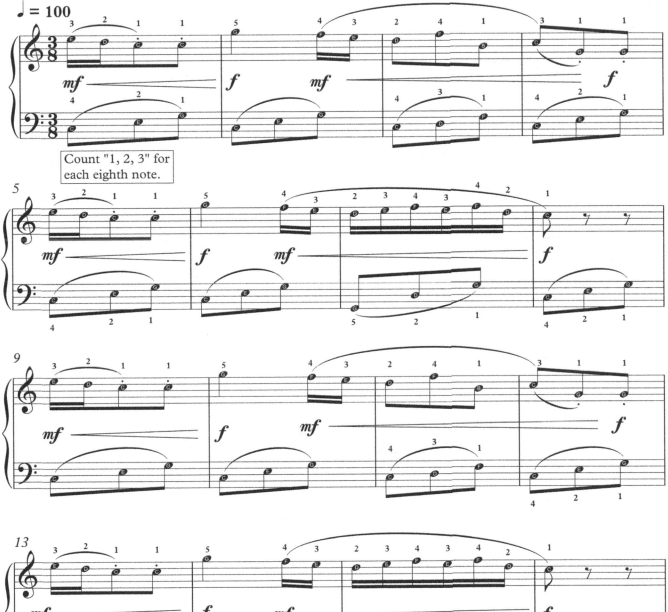

Count "1, 2, 3" for each eighth note.

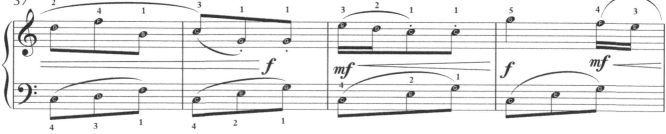

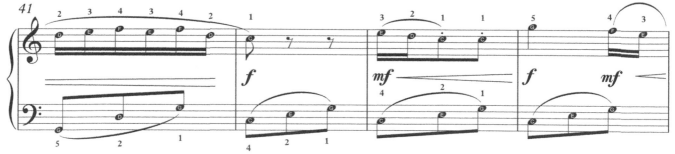

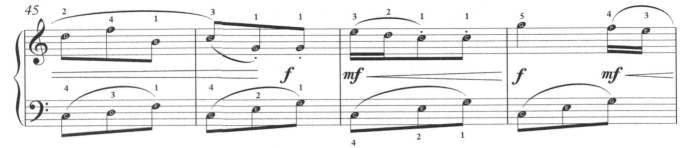

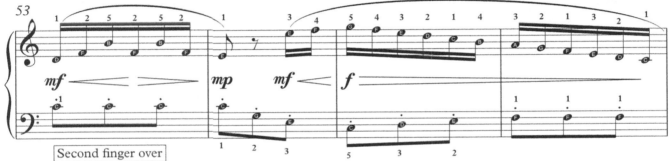

Second finger over

Second finger over

William Tell Overture
(Theme from the Lone Ranger)

Gioachino Rossini

For these two measures, count: 1 & 2 & a.

For this measure, in the left hand, count: 1 & 2 & a.

For this measure, in the left hand, count: 1 & 2 & a.

Hold this G major chord for three measures. Count: 1 & 2 &, 1 & 2 &, 1 & 2 &.

For this measure, count: 1 & 2 & a.

The Main Theme Returns

Congratulations!

Great work in completing this book and streaming video course on beginner classical piano! You now have an understanding of the fundamentals of piano playing: basic piano technique, beginner-level note reading and chord playing, and some understanding of music fundamentals–such as time signatures, beats, and the grand staff. As well, you have a repertoire of pieces to perform for family and friends!

Keep up the good work and continue to practice and play the piano!

Damon Ferrante

About the Author

Widely regarded among professional musicians, teachers, and students for his books' power to inspire a deeper understanding and passion for music, Damon Ferrante is a composer, guitarist, and professor of piano studies and music theory. He is the recipient of Longwood University's prestigious Simkins Award for his extraordinary achievements and contribution to music education and culture. Damon has taught on the music faculties of Seton Hall University and Montclair State University. For over 25 years, Damon has taught guitar, piano, composition, and music theory.

Damon has had performances at Carnegie Hall, Symphony Space, and throughout the US, Europe, and Asia. His main teachers have been David Rakowski at Columbia University, Stanley Wolfe at Juilliard, and Bruno Amato at the Peabody Conservatory of Johns Hopkins University. Damon has written two operas, a guitar concerto, song cycles, orchestral music, and numerous solo and chamber music works. He is the editor-in-chief of the music publisher Steeplechase Arts.

Check out steeplechasemusic.com for more information and free bonus lessons for the books.

Learn Piano
Scales, Chords & Technique!

Piano Scales Chords
Arpeggios Lessons

Book & Videos   Damon Ferrante

with Elements of Basic Music Theory

Learn How To Read Music!

Little Piano Book

Fun, Easy, Step-By-Step, Teach-Yourself Song and Beginner Piano Guide (Book & Streaming Videos) For All Ages!

No Music Reading Required!

by Damon Ferrante

Learn How To Play The Guitar!

Guitar Adventures
Teach Yourself How to Play Guitar for Beginners: Book & Streaming Videos

New Edition with 101 Lessons!

No Music Reading Required!

Damon Ferrante
Fun, Informative & Step-By-Step, Lesson Guide to Guitar
Beginner & Intermediate Levels (Book & Streaming Videos)

Learn Guitar
Scales, Chords & Technique!

Ultimate Guitar
Chords, Scales & Arpeggios
Handbook

240 Lessons For All Levels: Book & Streaming
Video Course by Damon Ferrante

Learn How To Play Rock Guitar!

Beginner Rock Guitar Lessons

Book & Videos — Damon Ferrante

Guitar Instruction Guide to Learn How to Play Licks, Chords, Scales, Techniques, Lead & Rhythm Guitar, Basic Music Theory, and Exercises - Teach Yourself or Work with an Instructor (Book, Videos & TAB)

Learn Guitar Scales!

Guitar Scales Handbook

New Edition with 100 Bonus Lessons!

A Step-By-Step, 100-Lesson Guide to Scales, Music Theory, and Fretboard Theory (Book & Videos)
Damon Ferrante

We want to help you become the pianist of your dreams!

Check Out Steeplechasemusic.com for Free Piano Lessons in Your Inbox!